EUROPE'S   HOPE

ALLIANCES

the answer to authocratic systems

and dictatorships

Contents

1. PERSPECTIVES

If we are to divide the world, as the international community sometimes prefers, then let it be in alliances. That would make it safer. Alliances can indeed bring stability and security when well-designed, as they facilitate the exchange of resources, knowledge, and support. Through alliances, different perspectives and expertise can be brought together, leading to innovative solutions and stronger cohesion. Moreover, alliances can help build trust and reduce conflicts by fostering a sense of belonging and solidarity. However, it is important that such alliances are based on principles of equality and respect. If certain groups dominate or exclude others, it will cause tensions and injustices. Therefore, the focus should be on creating inclusive and just alliances that recognize and value the diversity of voices and perspectives.

It is truly fascinating to further develop the idea of

alliances in this context. Well-constructed alliances can be a great source of power when properly utilized. Different communities, nations or political units support each other instead of retreating into isolation. In a world that is increasingly interconnected, cooperation and collaboration are more important than ever, especially in areas like technology, science, climate protection, and global security. By pooling resources and expertise, politics, economics, and research could respond more efficiently and effectively to the major challenges we face.

When alliances are based solely on an "us versus them"-mentality, they inevitably end up dividing the world into "us" and "them", the inevitable breeding ground for conflict. It is therefore crucial that such alliances are inclusive and recognize the diversity of perspectives and voices. If successful, they could not only lead to greater security and prosperity, but also create a deeper connection between continents.

If the alliance is to be successful, it needs clearly defined strategies that connect all partners. This requires transparent and continuous communication that keeps everyone up to date and addresses misunderstandings or conflicts at an early stage. This communication should not only discuss the common goals and strategies, but also the difficulties that could arise and how these can be addressed collectively. It's not just about the what, but also about the how.

Deep alliances must therefore be more than mere formal partnerships. They must include a genuine commitment to collaboration, equality and respectful communication. And even if the common goal is clear, it must never be forgotten that the way to get there is just as important as the goal itself. Only when the strategies, values and interests of all partners are respected will alliances be successful.

2. WHAT HAS BECOME OBSOLETE?

As the geopolitical landscape changes rapidly, so does the importance of alliances. Institutions that were once considered powerful players may have lost relevance in today's world. Changing political realities, fluctuating economic interests or new threats mean that they lose their impact if they are not re-set. Institutions that lose their relevance lose their ability to influence decisions or to drive change. This particularly affects international organizations, governments or large companies that have been considered driving forces for decades.If they are unable to adapt to new political, economic or technological realities, they lose influence and are overtaken by new players.This shift entails a redistribution of resources, power and influence.

Recognizing this and taking early action is crucial to avoid negative consequences. Delayed action in a political context ends in unstable situations that are associated with enormous costs and a high level of risk. In this respect, the timely recognition of changes is not only a question of reaction speed but also one of foresight. It requires managers who think flexibly, see change as an opportunity and are prepared to make sometimes difficult decisions before it is too late. The necessary adaptation is often precisely what is missing, even when all the signs point to change. Those in positions of power often only seem to react when the baby has long since fallen into the well. This late reaction, accompanied by the fear of taking responsibility, has tragic consequences.

The idea of sitting down at a table with presumptive partners and finding solutions together is considered too risky. Instead, the strategy of acting in isolation is being pursued: if we ignore all the problems, perhaps they will solve themselves! Why deal with the major geopolitical challenges when you can simply remain in fear? Powers such as China, Russia and recently the USA will only give in at some point, if Europe remains in its paralysis of fear. Wouldbe much better to rely on isolated solutions that no one really understands, but at least you can be sure that no one will get involved. Why invest in cooperative, multilateral approaches if you simply wait for everything to sort itself out somehow? It is much easier to switch to crisis mode and hope that the world will stabilize on its own, while Europe sits quietly in the corner and waits for the next big moment.

Would it be better to rely on special solutions that no one really understands? But at least you can be sure that no one will interfere. Why invest in cooperative, multilateral approaches if you just wait for everything to sort itself out? It's much easier to switch to crisis mode and hope that the world stabilizes on its own while Europe sits quietly in the corner, waiting for the next big moment.It has certainly become much more serious. Instead of remaining in fear and plunging into self-isolation, Europe could finally pluck up the courage to face up to the geopolitical challenges. Instead of pursuing isolated and ineffective solutions that are nothing more than political posturing, Europe should finally realize that dialogue and cooperation with partners are crucial to playing on the global stage. At a time when China, Russia and the USA are clearly defending their interests, Europe could take a clear stance and not constantly run after the big powers. You won't win the trust of the population and international partners by constantly ducking away. Europe must finally take bold, decisive steps, otherwise it will remain a mere spectator on the world stage in the long term.

Many countries are experiencing a resurgence of nationalism, leading to policies that prioritize domestic interests over international cooperation. This could result in enlarged protectionism and a decline in global trade. Ongoing conflicts and rivalries, such as those between major powers like the U.S. and China, could escalate, leading to a more fragmented world where alliances shift and international norms are challenged.

Growing income inequality within and between

countries can fuel discontent and instability, prompting countries to retreat into more insular policies that resist global interdependence. Advances in technology might change the dynamics of power, with countries that can harness new technologies gaining significant advantages, potentially leading to tensions and realignments. Climate change and resource scarcity could exacerbate geopolitical tensions, as nations compete for dwindling resources, leading to conflicts that disrupt global trade and cooperation. Each of these factors could contribute to a shift away from the interconnectedness that has characterized the globalized world, potentially leading to a more fragmented and less cooperative international environment.

The world is much more multipolar than it was just a few decades ago. While the Cold War divided the geopolitical landscape into two large blocs, we are now witnessing the emergence of several global powers that increasingly want to determine the political agenda. NATO, once conceived primarily as a military bulwark against the

Soviet threat, is struggling to redefine itself in the multipolar world. China and Russia, two powerful players, are increasingly taking an antagonistic stance towards Western institutions, creating a new area of tension. If NATO does not adapt and fails to build new security concepts and partnerships in the global arena, the consequences could be fatal.

In recent years, Russia and China have developed increasingly closer cooperation, particularly in response to Western policies. Both countries view themselves as a counterbalance to Western influence and advocate for a multipolar world order. They conduct joint military exercises, including air and naval maneuvers. This cooperation strengthens their military presence in key regions, such as the Pacific and the South China Sea.

Iran and North Korea also share a critical stance toward Western influence and have experienced sanctions and isolation by the West. North Korea benefits from Russian military resources and is a strategic partner for Russia in

East Asia. Iran and Russia collaborated in the defense industry, particularly in the context of the Syrian conflict, where both countries support the government of Bashar al-Assad.

China is the main trading partner for Russia and Iran. Especially after Western sanctions against Russia and Iran, these countries have increasingly sought trade relations with China. China purchases large amounts of energy and builds infrastructure projects in these countries. North Korea is economically dependent on China, although it does not have the same level of close economic cooperation as the other countries. North Korea receives support in the form of food and fuel, which is provided by China. China and Russia support Iran diplomatically and militarily, particularly regarding Iran's nuclear program and the geopolitical situation in the Middle East. These countries have often coordinated to bypass Western sanctions. For example, China has repeatedly vetoed United Nations sanctions against Iran and North Korea and, to some extent, continued trade.

A new Atlantic-Pacific alliance could effectively counter the growing cooperation between Russia, China, Iran and North Korea by developing a cohesive strategy that includes military deterrence, diplomatic measures, economic policies and technological advancements. Such an alliance would need to focus on strengthening defense capabilities, enhancing economic ties, and leveraging diplomatic influence to challenge the geopolitical and strategic efforts of these countries.

On the economic stage, countries such as China have expanded their economic power and now dominate many industrial and technological sectors. At the same time, many Western economies are experiencing economic stagnation and a suspicious loss of competitiveness. ASEAN, the Association of Southeast Asian Nations, has also lost influence as China has increasingly emerged as the dominant power in the region. The member states are faced with the challenge of finding a balance between cooperation with China and their traditional Western partners. The growing economic dependence on China and the increasing divergence of economic interests within ASEAN are weakening the entire region.

Many countries are questioning the traditional economic blocs and looking for new economic models that offer more flexibility. The traditional threats to global security, such as the danger of direct military conflict between major powers, are no longer the only relevant aspects today. Instead, new, transnational risks and threats have come to the fore that are difficult to address by existing alliances. These include cyber attacks, climate change, terrorism, pandemics and humanitarian crises.

Comprehensive reforms within the existing institutions could improve the ability to act through restructuring. However, this would require a rapid change of heart with courage and a great deal of initiative. The irony is that the very institutions that see themselves as stable and fit for the future often fail to develop the necessary flexibility due to their rigidity and adherence to old structures. A bit like a ship that stubbornly heads for the iceberg, even though it is already visible in the distance. And in the end, the question arises: "Why didn't we see this earlier?"

Established political and economic leaders must have the courage to challenge entrenched ways of thinking and actively drive change. Many existing international organizations are hampered by slow bureaucratic processes and inefficient decision-making structures. These structures need to be redesigned so that decisions are made in real time and based on up-to-date data, without always having to wait for consensus from all members.

Reforms must focus on greater transparency and accountability in decision-making processes. Today's global institutions often face accusations of a lack of transparency, which leads to a loss of trust. To remain credible, these institutions would need to develop clear mechanisms for participation, influence and accountability. If this change of heart does not take place, it could be said that the institutions will continue to dwell in their familiar twilight zone of bureaucracies, a perfect backdrop to stage the spectacle of a fake globality while the world outside is changing.

Reforms should aim to make the decision-making processes of these institutions clear and understandable. This means that all involved actors, whether states, organizations, or citizens must be included in the processes and should have influence over the decisions. In order to remain truly credible, these institutions would need to create structures that allow stakeholders to actively participate, exert influence, and hold the institutions accountable.

If these reforms are not implemented, there is a risk that the institutions will continue to stagnate in a bureaucratic state. This bureaucracy would keep the institutions in a state of inaction and immutability, while the world outside continues to evolve. As a result, the institutions would no longer respond to the real, dynamic challenges but would only maintain a false world of global collaboration.

The term "false globality" refers to the fact that these institutions may give the impression of acting globally and being an integral part of global cooperation, but in reality, they do not engage with or address the current challenges and changes in the world. This would lead to a disconnected portrayal of progress and cooperation, while the real problems and changes outside of these institutions continue to exist.

The stage is set. In such a scenario, one could admire the UN Security Council as the masterpiece of standstill art, where veto rights are still as impressive as ancient relics on display in the museum room of geopolitical significance. At the same time, the World Bank sits in a glass office and has a permanent staff that knows exactly how to shred paper in a digital world to simulate the feeling of productivity. ASEAN, meanwhile, could get lost in an endless loop that, instead of actual action, ends up in more meetings until the next diplomatic incident in the South China Sea arrives and no one can really do anything because multilateralism is stuck in a holding pattern.

3. NEW AXES

China and Russia intend to challenge and replace the old political and military structures. The joint declaration between China and Russia on February 4, 2022 shows a clear rejection of the traditional systems that were established primarily during the Cold War and afterwards. The partnership between China and Russia is specifically directed against Western dominance in international politics. Both countries conduct joint military exercises, including air and naval maneuvers. This cooperation strengthens their military presence in key regions, such as the Pacific and the South China Sea. Iran and North Korea also share a critical stance toward Western influence, and have experienced sanctions and isolation by the West. North Korea benefits from Russian military resources and is a strategic partner for Russia in East Asia.

China and Russia are increasingly pursuing the goal of

challenging the existing political and military structures of the post-war order and replacing them with a new, multi-polar system. This old order, which emerged after the Second World War under the influence of the United States and its Western allies, is based on institutions such as NATO, the United Nations, the World Bank and the International and trade system, all structures based on Western values such as democracy, the rule of law and a liberal market economy. However, China and Russia increasingly see this order as a system that limits their own security and economic interests.

China relies primarily on economic and technological power to gain global influence. With the Belt and Road Initiative it invests in infrastructure projects around the world, creating new dependencies, especially in the global south. At the same time, China is expanding its military presence in the Indo-Pacific region, especially in the South China Sea and towards Taiwan. China is also creating alternative power centers in the digital space by establishing its own standards in telecommunications, artificial intelligence and internet surveillance. The aim is to reduce the technological dependence on the West in the long term and at the same time to impose its own standards globally.

Russia, on the other hand, has a more confrontational strategy. The annexation of Crimea in 2014 and the attack on Ukraine from 2022 mark open military challenges to the Western security order. In addition, Russia uses disinformation campaigns and cyber attacks to destabilize Western societies and undermine confidence in democratic institutions. On the international level, Russia is increasingly seeking strategic alliances, be it with China, Iran or North Korea and trying to create geopolitical leverage through energy policy, especially control over gas supplies to Europe. Both countries are also working to supplement or replace Western-dominated institutions with their own formats. Examples are the creation of alternatives to the World Bank by the Asian Infrastructure Investment Bank or joint military exercises within the framework of the

Shanghai Cooperation Organization.

China is the main trading partner for Russia and Iran. Especially after Western sanctions against Russia and Iran, these countries have increasingly sought trade relations with China. China purchases large amounts of energy and builds infrastructure projects in these countries. North Korea is economically dependent on China, although it does not have the same level of close economic cooperation as the other countries. North Korea receives support in the form of food and fuel, which is provided by China. China and Russia support Iran diplomatically and militarily, particularly regarding Iran's nuclear program and the geopolitical situation in the Middle East. These countries have often coordinated to bypass Western sanctions. For example, China has repeatedly vetoed United Nations sanctions against Iran and North Korea and, to some extent, continued trade.

A new Atlantic-Pacific alliance could effectively counter the growing cooperation between Russia, China, Iran and North Korea by developing a cohesive strategy that includes military deterrence, diplomatic measures, economic policies and technological advancements. Such an alliance would need to focus on strengthening defense capabilities, enhancing economic ties, and leveraging diplomatic influence to challenge the geopolitical and strategic efforts of these countries.

Why is Russian disinformation so effective in the countries of the Global South? Russia promotes narratives that portray the West as imperialist or hypocritical, while positioning itself as a partner in opposition to the West. These platforms are often less regulated, which makes it easier for Russian disinformation networks to spread false or manipulative content. In countries with lower media literacy and institutional resources, people are often more susceptible to fake news and propaganda. Russia deliberately exploits the divisions in these insecure societies to extend social polarization and further destabilize societies.

Russia has received support from China with regard to the Ukraine conflict and Western sanctions. Conversely, China benefits from Russia's support with regard to security policy issues and its growing military influence in Central Asia. Iran is actively involved in regional conflicts and uses proxy wars to expand its influence in the Middle East. North Korea remains an isolated actor, often using nuclear threats and aggressive rhetoric.

Russia and China have recently carried out repeated cyberattacks on military and economic targets. These tactics make it possible to destabilize critical infrastructure, steal strategic information or influence political processes. These powers rely on disinformation to manipulate public opinion in other countries, promote political instability and undermine the credibility of Western institutions. Russia is a particularly active player here, especially in the context of elections and democratic processes in Western countries.

The commercialization of power also threatens

international stability by putting economic interests and personal profits above values such as cooperation and global responsibility. Populist figures such as Donald Trump with his administration team in the US exacerbate this dynamic through their isolationist stance and mistrust of international alliances, which undermines global cooperation. In the face of these challenges, the international community needs to find new ways to respond to threats. In particular, rapid, coordinated action in business and research and the development of economic partnerships based on shared values and fair trade practices could create new, stronger cooperation. The promotion of regional economies and the decentralization of power could provide more stable and resilient alternatives in the long term.

In the long term, the preservation of the world order can only succeed if a value-based order is promoted and strengthened globally. Education, cultural exchange and support for civil society initiatives could help more countries to identify with these values and counter unfair attempts to destabilize the order. The preservation of the world order will indeed rely heavily on the promotion and strengthening of a value-based system that transcends borders. A world order that is anchored in shared values such as peace, human rights, democracy, and sustainability has the potential to create a more resilient global community, capable of withstanding challenges and countering destabilizing forces.

Overall, it is a combination of preventive measures, international cooperation and a strong defense that is necessary to safeguard the existing international peace and order. It is fundamentally determining to be flexible and responsive to new threats. Indeed, the world order is at a turning point where the creation of new alliances of resistance against an increasingly isolationist and self-interested imperialist tendency offers a unique opportunity in new guises.

The current geopolitical shift opens up the possibility of forging alternative alliances that do not rely on the traditional superpowers. Instead, the focus could be on countries and regions that are committed to open, inclusive and cooperative principles. Focusing on joint economic partnerships and interdisciplinary research initiatives could lay the foundations for a more resilient formation. Such alliances offer not only economic benefits, but also solutions to global challenges such as climate change or pandemics. Global economic decentralization could free countries from dependence on a few superpowers. Regional alliances could react more stably and flexibly to global pressure and create innovative models of cooperation.

4. HOW ABOUT AN „APTO"?

A global pact such as an Atlantic Pacific Treaty Organization could indeed be a visionary and powerful step towards ushering in a new era of global cooperation. Such a treaty would combine the strengths of existing transatlantic potentials, for example with Canada and Pacific alliances, but also create new partnerships based not only on military security, but also on shared political, economic and social values. By integrating nations from both the Atlantic and Pacific realms, this treaty could foster a more balanced, interconnected approach to global governance, an alliance that is more representative of the 21st century's geopolitical realities.

Such an "APTO" could emerge as an institutionalized platform that addresses a broad range of global challenges, focusing not only on military security, but also on geopolitical cooperation, economic partnership, scientific research and global sustainability. This alliance could bring together Europe, the North of America, Asia and Pacific states to work together on a cooperative world order without resorting to hegemonic claims to power or isolationism. The result would be a very effective formation in the fight against the increasingly globally networked clouds of dictatorships, which are spreading ever further and forming ever more powerful networks. The APTO could stand as a beacon for democratic values, human rights and rule of law, offering a counterbalance to authoritarian regimes that are gaining influence on the world stage.

APTO could serve as a counterweight to this authoritarian surge by uniting like-minded democracies, enhancing cooperation in areas like digital governance, supply chain security, and defense, and by offering meaningful support to nations at risk of falling under authoritarian sway. Its legitimacy, however, would depend not only on shared strategic interests but on a genuine commitment to upholding the principles it claims to defend. In a world increasingly shaped by power politics and spheres of influence, the formation of such an alliance could represent a critical step toward preserving a rules-based, open and pluralistic international system.

Another significant aspect could be an enhanced focus on environmental security, with countries from the Atlantic and Pacific regions cooperating to fight climate change, protect oceans, and share green technologies. This would not only serve global interests but also resonate with the younger generations who view climate change as one of the most pressing issues of their time.

In essence, an Atlantic Pacific Treaty Organization could be a bold step toward creating a unified, multipolar world that values shared democratic principles, economic integration, cultural exchange, and collective responsibility for global security. The success of such an initiative would rely heavily on the commitment of member states to mutual respect, understanding, and a vision of a peaceful, prosperous global future.

Without being specific, the geographical arc of a "horseshoe" could extend from South America, with Brazil as its epicenter, via Mexico north to Canada and Europe. There the curve bends towards the Asian continent, whether with the UAE, India, Taiwan, South Korea, Japan or Australia is largely open. This idea of a geographical arc for an Atlantic Pacific Treaty Organization is exciting geopolitically and strategically, as it would unite a large number of important players in a comprehensive network. The geographical arc could serve as a kind of global cooperation zone, bringing together not only Western democracies but also important Asian nations. After all, Europe's interests are not that far removed from securing East Asian trade routes and waterways. And they all have specific interests and needs that should not be underestimated.

Brazil would be the epicenter of South American cooperation in this arc. As the continent's largest economy and a country with an important geopolitical role in the southern hemisphere, Brazil could build a bridge between the western and South American regions. Greater cooperation with Europe and Asia could strengthen Brazilian initiatives in the areas of environmental protection, agriculture and technology. Brazil desperately needs internal and external stabilization. For Mexico, as for Canada, the unpredictable USA has long been a risk factor. Europe's risk factor, on the other hand, is Russia and, subsequently, China and, more recently, the USA. China is India's risk factor, as it is for Taiwan, South Korea and Japan. All the units cited are located in clearly defined risk clouds and would have a considerable interest in participating in security. The emphasis on the collective approach should be emphasized, as many of these risks cannot be managed by a single country alone.

The security architecture coincide with economic relations and free trade. Large-scale research networks are also an important linchpin for intensive cooperation.

This not only promotes the exchange of knowledge, but also innovation, which is of crucial importance for the security and prosperity of many countries. The intertwining of security architecture, economic relations, and free trade can create a robust framework that promotes stability and growth. When nations cooperate on security, it sets the foundation for deeper, long-lasting economic ties, creating an environment of trust and mutual benefit.

Europe is well positioned with its internal balance of tasks in large regions that still need to be organized. This makes Europe a hoped-for hub of global security and prosperity. It strengthens the ability to further expand the European economic and security architecture through innovative and sustainable initiatives. This includes not only the coordination of trade agreements and investments, but also the development of security and defense cooperation that positions Europe as a stable player in an increasingly multipolar world. Europe could also benefit from a more active engagement in areas such as digitalization, green technologies and global health strategies, as these fields not only stimulate economic growth but also demonstrate strategic advantages in terms of global security. Europe's strategic position and its internal cohesion make it a strong contender to play a leading role in shaping the future of global security and prosperity. As the world becomes more multipolar, Europe is uniquely poised to balance competing interests, create synergies between various regions, and strengthen its economic and security frameworks. Europe's influence will only grow if it actively engages in key sectors that are critical for economic prosperity and security on a global scale.

Europe is at a critical juncture, where its internal balance of tasks and its focus on innovation, sustainability, and security could set it on a path toward becoming a central hub of global prosperity and stability. Through strategic engagement in digitalization, green technologies, and global health, Europe can solidify its role as a key player in the multipolar world. The expansion of Europe's economic and security frameworks will ensure its resilience in the face of global challenges, and its leadership in these critical sectors will continue to drive regional and global cooperation.

This would allow it to perfect not only its economic engine, but also its stabilizing position in the international security architecture. Europe would be ill-advised not to seize these opportunities and invest more in multilateral initiatives and partnerships with other global players. Europe should take full advantage of this geopolitical freedom and position itself as an independent and strong player in global politics. A club of the willing that combines technology, security and sustainable development could create the basis for an innovative and sustainable Europe. Conversely, an overly hesitant, incoherent stance would only weaken the EU in the long term and set it back in a geopolitical environment dominated by other major players.

Parallel to these collaborations, the straightforward

exchange of trade and cooperation with the neighboring continent of Africa should not be overlooked. The geographical proximity and economic links between Europe and Africa offer enormous potential for closer cooperation. Africa will be one of the fastest growing economic regions in the world in the coming decades, with a young, dynamic population and enormous potential in various sectors, from agriculture and resources to technology and infrastructure.

The relationship between Europe and Africa offers a wealth of untapped potential that could be harnessed through closer economic and trade cooperation. The geographical proximity, coupled with shared historical and cultural ties, presents a strong foundation for deeper collaboration that benefits both continents. Europe, with its established infrastructure, financial systems, and technology, is well-positioned to be a primary partner for Africa's transformation. Strategic economic cooperation, especially in sectors where Europe has significant expertise, could help unlock

Africa's potential while creating new opportunities for European businesses.

Africa has vast agricultural potential, with arable land that could feed not only its own population but also contribute to global food security. However, challenges like outdated farming techniques, lack of infrastructure, and climate change impact have hindered Africa's ability to fully capitalize on its agricultural potential. European expertise in sustainable agriculture, precision farming, and supply chain logistics could help Africa modernize its agricultural sector. Joint ventures and technology transfers could improve yields, reduce food waste, and create more resilient food systems. Additionally, Africa's growing agricultural sector could serve as a valuable source of exports for European markets, particularly in areas such as fresh produce, coffee, cocoa, and textiles.

Africa is rich in natural resources, including minerals, oil, gas, and precious metals. However, the challenge for many African nations is ensuring that these resources are developed sustainably, with local economies benefiting from their extraction and export, while minimizing environmental harm. Europe, with its leadership in environmental sustainability and green technologies, could partner with African countries to develop their natural resources in a responsible manner. By introducing clean energy solutions, such as solar, wind, and hydropower, Europe could help Africa reduce its dependence on fossil fuels and create more sustainable growth pathways.

The technology sector in Africa is growing rapidly, particularly in mobile technology, fintech, and digital services. Many African nations have leapfrogged traditional infrastructure by adopting mobile phones and digital solutions at a much faster rate than some developed countries.Europe can play a pivotal role by fostering technological innovation and helping to develop Africa's digital infrastructure. Initiatives in areas like e-commerce, mobile banking, and digital education could be expanded through European investment and collaboration. Europe's tech companies can also work with African startups to exchange knowledge, while also contributing to the development of digital skills, enabling a digital economy that is inclusive and sustainable.

An alliance between African tech hubs and Europe could be a powerful partnership that fosters mutual growth, innovation, and development. Given the rapid growth of Africa's tech scene, especially in cities like Cape Town, Johannesburg, and Nairobi, this alliance could open up several avenues for collaboration and shared opportunities. By partnering, both continents could share best practices, knowledge, and innovations that could accelerate growth in both markets. This could involve joint R&D projects focused on sustainable technology, climate change, healthcare, and more. The collaboration could involve leveraging Europe's advanced tech and Africa's experience in deploying tech solutions in resource-constrained environments.

Africa faces significant challenges in infrastructure development, from roads and railways to energy grids and telecommunications. At the same time, the African Union's Agenda 2063 highlights infrastructure as one of the continent's top priorities, with ambitious plans for regional integration and development. Europe can contribute by investing in key infrastructure projects, such as transport corridors, renewable energy facilities, and smart cities. Europe's expertise in urban planning, construction, and sustainable development could help African countries build the infrastructure necessary to support their growing populations and economies. In turn, these investments will open new markets for European businesses, particularly in construction, energy, and technology.

Europe could benefit from this development by strengthening trade relations, investing in infrastructure and technology development and expanding partnerships in education and innovation. Such cooperation would not only facilitate access to new markets and resources, but would also increase prosperity and economic development on the African continent.

One of Africa's greatest assets is its young population, but unlocking their potential requires investment in education and skills development. Europe can assist by providing access to quality education, vocational training, and capacity-building programs. Collaborative programs between European and African universities and institutions could provide young Africans with the skills needed to thrive in a global economy. Similarly, European businesses could partner with African companies to offer on-the-job training and internships, equipping the next generation of African workers with the experience necessary for success.

Sustainability should be at the heart of any European-African partnership. As both continents face environmental challenge, such as climate change and the need for green energy solutions, their cooperation in sustainable development initiatives could set a global example. For example, Europe could work with Africa to support the transition to green energy, with a focus on renewable energy projects like solar and wind farms. At the same time, Europe could help African nations manage natural resources sustainably, ensuring that economic growth does not come at the cost of environmental degradation.

Closer cooperation between Europe and Africa could also have important geopolitical ramifications. By building strong, mutually beneficial relationships with African countries, Europe can help strengthen African institutions and promote regional stability. In turn, this would reduce the potential for conflicts, migration crises, and instability that could have far-reaching impacts on Europe. Africa's role in global geopolitics is growing, especially as it plays a key part in the shift toward a multipolar world. By engaging more deeply with Africa, Europe can help shape a more balanced, stable international order.

The time is ripe for a more integrated, dynamic partnership between Europe and Africa, one that recognizes the immense potential of Africa's youth, resources, and markets while ensuring that growth is sustainable and inclusive. By working together, Europe and Africa can become powerful drivers of global change, positioning both continents for success in the coming decades.

Europe's response to Africa's needs in terms of infrastructure development, technology, and green energy could evolve over time, shaped by Africa's changing priorities and challenges. By continuously engaging in dialogue and responding to the evolving needs of its partners, Europe can ensure that its cooperation remains relevant, effective, and beneficial.

It is important for Europe to emphasize that it does not see itself at the top, but rather as a coveted pivot around which so much revolves. Such a role as mediator and coordinator is not only diplomatically skillful, but also more successful in the long term. By acting as an active and flexible partner that stimulates dialog and cooperation, Europe can play a key role both in Africa and on the global stage. By acting as an equal partner rather than a dominant leader, Europe will build trust and create deeper, authentic relationships. This not only enhances long-term alliances, but also maximizes sustainable mutual development. This attitude emphasizes respectful dialogue and responsibility sharing, which encourages a stronger political and economic partnership.

Europe's strength lies in its ability to bring together different actors with varied interests. In a multipolar world, where power dynamics are shifting and regional priorities often diverge, Europe's ability to mediate and coordinate is a unique asset. As a mediator, Europe can facilitate dialogue and offer platforms for conflict resolution that allow for compromises and shared solutions, rather than imposing unilateral decisions. This is particularly critical in regions like Africa, where diverse political, social, and economic contexts require nuanced approaches.

Trust is a key element in any successful partnership. To build trust, Europe must engage in respectful dialogue, which includes actively listening to the concerns and priorities of its partners, especially in Africa. This means engaging in discussions that go beyond economic interests, and that are grounded in a deep understanding of the unique social, cultural, and political landscapes of each partner.

Europe's willingness to listen and act as a responsible partner will not only deepen its relationships with African countries but also elevate its reputation globally as a mediator that prioritizes fairness, equality, and cooperation. This is particularly important in the context of global governance, where Europe's credibility can be strengthened by demonstrating its commitment to promoting a just and inclusive world order.

The goal of any partnership should be mutual development, a growth that benefits both parties in the long term. The concept of mutual development is a defining feature of a truly sustainable and impactful partnership. This stands in stark contrast to the approaches taken by other global powers such as Russia and China, which often pursue partnerships driven by asymmetrical benefits, where the growth or gain of one party, usually the more dominant, comes at the expense of the other.

Europe's commitment to sustainable development can play a central role in ensuring that its partnerships with Africa and other regions are not only economically viable but also socially and environmentally responsible. Europe has the tools and expertise to promote sustainable business practices, renewable energy solutions, and environmentally-friendly technologies that can drive growth while preserving natural resources.

By acting as a neutral facilitator, Europe can help manage complex global issues like migration, security, climate change, and economic inequality, ensuring that all parties involved feel heard and valued. This would not only improve Europe's influence but also ensure that solutions are more inclusive, balanced, and long-lasting. By prioritizing mutual development and respecting sovereignty, Europe can strengthen its diplomatic leverage and expand its influence globally. Rather than relying on coercion or economic pressure, as sometimes seen in Chinese or Russian dealings, Europe can create a network of like-minded partners who trust its intentions and view it as a reliable, responsible partner. This will enhance European soft power and foster strategic partnerships based on shared values such as democracy, rule of law, and human rights.

Europe would have the prerequisites in areas such as science, education, culture and technology to stimulate exchange by acting as a hub for research networks, educational initiatives or digital platforms. Such initiatives not only mobilize alliance relations, but also contribute to the creation of a broadly coordinated counter-front to existing over-dominant clouds such as in Silicon Valley. This would not only strengthen Europe's role in global leadership but also help shape a more diverse, inclusive, and resilient digital and research-driven future.

The idea of Silicon Valley as a centralized hub of global tech development has raised concerns about the concentration of power in the hands of a few tech giants. By positioning itself as a counterweight to this, Europe could offer a more diverse, inclusive and democratic approach to technology development. This can be achieved through the creation of European tech alliances, open-source collaboration, and the establishment of technology hubs that focus on public good rather than solely commercial profit. Moreover, by promoting transparency, accountability, and regulation within the tech industry, Europe could set global standards that counteract the unchecked power of global tech monopolies. This would not only boost Europe's digital sovereignty but also contribute to a more equitable and diverse digital economy. By leveraging its strength in these areas, Europe could create a network of mutual exchange that not only stimulates global partnerships but also provides a counterbalance to the existing dominant tech hubs in the USA. By prioritizing inclusive innovation, ethical technology, and open-access education, Europe can reshape the global landscape, fostering a more sustainable and collaborative future for all. This approach could serve as a powerful competitive advantage, offering Europe the opportunity to lead through responsibility, creativity, and mutual development.

Such a vertical alliance between African and Europe could not only be technologically and creatively enriching, but also make an important contribution to a global concept such as the ventured APCO - Africa and

Pacific Cooperation Organization. A broader partnership that encompasses technological innovation and economic cooperation could significantly strengthen the global framework for cooperation and sustainable development.

A strategic focus on technology and innovation promotion between Africa, Europe and the Pacific and the western part of the horseshoe in South America and the Americas could create synergies that drive development on multiple levels, from infrastructure to education to sustainable business.

An alliance within an APCO could enable African and Pacific countries, with support from the Atlantic flank, to further diversify their economies by opening up new markets for sustainable technologies and green innovations. Especially in a global context that is increasingly focusing on sustainability, the developments could serve as a model for sustainable and socially responsible business models.

Such a partnership could also have an impact on the educational landscape by establishing programs to promote and develop talent across borders. Colleges, universities and research institutions could cooperate in a joint network of APCO countries to develop educational initiatives that promote technological progress and social mobility.

An APCO that encompasses technological innovation and economic cooperation could serve as one of the most important platforms for global partnerships and development in the 21st century. Merging the creative, technological and economic strengths of Africa, Europe and the Pacific on the one hand and the Atlantic region on the other could not only lead to major economic growth, but also usher in a new era of cooperation and global knowledge exchange. The concept of such a cooperation provides an excellent basis for balancing any emerging weaknesses or disagreements on the one atlantic balance pan with immediate counter-initiatives on the pacific side, and vice versa.

Building such an alliance requires not only strategic planning, but also continuous communication, collaboration and finding compromises between the different parties. In a complex alliance, different interests, values and goals often need to be reconciled, which poses challenges. It also requires strong trust and clear leadership to unite the different players and make the alliance stable and effective in the long term.

5. A SECURITY ARCHITECTURE AND
   RESEARCH NETWORK

Internally, Europe already has many successful initiatives such as Horizon Europe, a major EU research and innovation program that helps promote scientific collaboration and technological innovation. However, to play a stronger role as a global hub for research and development, Europe could develop even more targeted international partnerships in key areas such as artificial intelligence, quantum computing, sustainability and health. These networks would not only accelerate the exchange of knowledge, but also ensure that Europe is perceived as a consumer of technology as well as an innovation coordinator.

Europe would position itself as a global education hub by combining educational programs and scholarship initiatives for international students, researchers and technology talent from Africa, Asia and other regions. Initiatives such as the Erasmus programmes have already successfully promoted international exchange programmes, but Europe could expand even further beyond its borders by not only promoting academic networks, but also supporting vocational and technological training in areas such as digitalization, artificial intelligence and sustainable technologies in the global alliance. The aim should be to create an international network of professionals and innovators trained in Europe while collaborating with other regions.

In order to act as an alternative source of innovation to the USA and China, Europe would have to rely more heavily on multinational technology alliances. This means that the EU, together with other partners, inside and outside Europe, develops its own technologies and standards that not only serve the European single market, but could be established as a global standard.

Another area in which Europe could act as a hub is the

development and dissemination of green technologies and sustainable innovations. GreenTech and Circular Economy initiatives are a key pillar for European partnerships. Europe is in a position not only to play a driving role in the research and development of innovative green technologies, but also to act as a marketplace for sustainable solutions that promote European and global development.

More than just a field for scientific discovery, space is a key element of the geopolitical and economic significance of a new kind of alliance. At a time when space technologies are increasingly the basis for innovation in areas such as communications, navigation, climate research and security, the new alliance should play an influential role through increased cooperation in the space sector.

Space technology could take on a significant strategic value for the new alliance and act as a kind of contrasting program to the existing superpowers of the

USA and China. This should be of great interest to India or the Southeast Asian technology giants in their geographical isolation. The dependence on the space infrastructures of the USA with "GPS", or China with "Beidou", represents a geopolitical risk. A stronger focus on the creation of an independent global space infrastructure could help to dynamize the Alliance's sovereignty and ability to act in space. By emphasizing multilateralism, peace, sustainability and economic cooperation, the new European alliance could develop an alternative, inclusive and value-based space strategy that is attractive for Europe itself and for its alliance partners.

However, the scale and complexity of the task requires not only a long-term plan, but also a coherent, coordinated effort at all levels: from political leaders to scientists, engineers and the general public. Europe could play an interesting mediating role here through a mix of visionary leadership, innovative partnerships and a clear multilateral strategy.

The decentralization of power and the promotion of regional economic areas are complex challenges that require support and cooperation not only at the political level, but also in society and in the economy. Political leadership should not only be able to articulate this vision, but also have the courage and wisdom to put it into practice, even if the political and economic challenges are enormous.

The challenges associated with decentralization can hardly be tackled by individual countries or players alone. Innovative partnerships are needed to create synergies and pool the necessary resources. Due to its unique structure as an association of many different states with different economic and political systems, Europe has a special opportunity here to act as a model for cooperation and collaboration. It could serve as a bridge between different interest groups and regions, helping to bring different perspectives together to find viable solutions. Europe could act as a mediator between global actors and regional interests while emphasizing the importance of local autonomy. Through multilateral forums and negotiations, common standards, solutions and measures could be developed that meet regional needs and global challenges.

For decentralization and the promotion of regional economies to be successful, a coordinated effort is required, from political leadership to scientific and technological research to the people on the ground who have to implement the changes. The general public has an essential role to play in accepting, supporting and actively shaping these changes. People need to understand why decentralization and the promotion of regional economies are important and how they can benefit from these changes. A clear communication approach that explains the benefits and necessity of this transformation is crucial to overcoming resistance and engaging the population.

Europe has a unique opportunity to act as a model for a successful combination of decentralized autonomy and overarching cooperation. The EU already has experience in coordinating between states with different economic, political and cultural systems. This experience could be used to support internal European regions as well as other parts of the world that want to tackle similar challenges.

A coherent, coordinated effort requires not only political and economic measures, but also long-term investment in education, research and innovation. Scientists and engineers are the engines that must find the practical solutions to the challenges of decentralization and regional development. It is therefore crucial to invest in a highly skilled and innovation-driven workforce to develop new technologies and solutions to support this transformation.

This means pursuing long-term visions that offer geopolitical and technological added value. They should not only fuel technological progress, but also keep the global partnership and cooperation networks on their toes. The Alliance should be wary of pursuing one-way technological paths with limited benefits and no broad international cooperation or application opportunities. The aim is to develop flexible, scalable technologies that are also compatible with other global players and enable multilateral partnerships. One example could be the development of open standards or interoperable satellite systems that are accessible not only to the specific alliance, but also to other countries.

The alliance should focus on ambitious long-term projects that have a global impact and stimulate international cooperation. Smaller, isolated projects should be avoided in order not to lose focus and then be overtaken by the leading competitors of the world powers. The key is for the Alliance to remain active in key leverage technologies and position itself as a strategic partner for many countries worldwide. Such an approach allows it to present itself as a hub for ideas and solutions, bringing together different stakeholders to tackle common challenges. The ability to build bridges and take into account the interests of different parties could be of crucial managerial importance.

6. NEW MANAGEMENT SKILLS IN POLITICS

What are the management skills of global alliances? Understanding how to communicate effectively with thinkers from different cultural backgrounds is on the agenda. This includes an overall sensitivity to the diversity of cultures and norms. The starting point is a feeling for the needs and interests of the partners. Co-creation begins with the formulation of strategic goals that benefit all partners. This still includes analyzing competitive conditions and trends.

In a constantly changing global environment, it is important to remain flexible, not to lose sight of the big picture and to constantly adapt to new conditions. This may require strategic and operational changes. Identifying and managing risks associated with international partnerships is a sensitive task. A strong network needs to be maintained in order to exchange information, receive support and identify new developments. It will require a deep understanding of the specific markets in which the partners operate. Only then will decisions be made that are capable of taking advantage of opportunities. The ability to maintain and develop these relationships is the engine of the spiral forward.

The concept of political management in the context of a new alliance dedicated to fighting against the supremacy of violence is a very profound and challenging subject. This is not only about strategic cooperation between different players, but also about creating a stable framework that aims at long-term conflict resolution, peaceful coexistence and the promotion of security and justice. Such an alliance requires precise and sensitive political leadership.

The strategy of strength and justice is a concept that combines the use of power and the maintenance of moral and ethical principles. It is about using assertiveness as a means to ensure justice without falling into authoritarian or violent practices. The implementation of such a political management concept involves the principles of conceptuality and evaluation, reactive rationality, perspectivity and urgency, all of which provide the problem-centred stimuli. The strength of such a strategy means at the same time military and economic power. The ability to act decisively in difficult situations is called for, but strength must be used responsibly. Instead of simply exercising power, it must be used to correct injustices and make the world order more stable. Justice is closely linked to the rule of law. A strategy of strength and justice is committed to ensuring that international standards are consistently enforced. This includes combating injustice as well as human rights violations, as well as supporting institutions that defend the rule of law.

These concepts are not merely theoretical considerations, but provide the basis for responding to global and societal challenges in a targeted and effective manner. They define the strategic direction to solve problems related to the supremacy of violence and injustice. The term refers to how problems and challenges that need to be addressed are defined. It influences the way in which these problems are perceived and how they are assessed, that is, what priorities are set and how solutions are formulated. A clear understanding and precise terminology are necessary to name the challenges correctly. In a political context, for example, this means defining precisely what is meant by the supremacy of violence or justice. Only precise terms can develop a coherent strategy that is comprehensible and applicable to all actors.

In a global management approach, it must be decided whether certain forms of violence are more urgent than others. For example, immediate intervention in a crisis region may be given higher weight than a long-term development strategy. Reactive rationality means reacting to events, developments or crises by evaluating the facts and data available quickly and sensibly. In a political management concept, this means responding quickly and appropriately to sudden conflicts, violent clashes or crises.

Perspectivity means to consider the long-term effects of decisions and not just focus on immediate responses. This refers to the forward-looking way of thinking and the ability to look at how policy measures and strategies are implemented from different angles. The perspectivity in a political management concept ensures that actions are in line with the overarching objectives. It ensures that the long-term consequences of decisions, such as the creation of stable societies or the sustainable promotion of the rule of law are also taken into account. A political strategy of strength must be able to respond to urgent humanitarian crises. Armed conflicts, genocide or large-scale human rights violations are the top priorities. The ability to act quickly and effectively at such critical moments is crucial for minimizing damage and steering the course towards a more just and peaceful future.

The concept of problem-centered stimuli refers to the dynamic responses that are necessary to solve the most pressing problems in a global context. In a political management concept, these stimuli are controlled by clear problem analyses and objectives that come into play in the responsiveness just like in the preventive planning. Problem-centred stimuli require a continuous analysis of the global situation and the rapid identification of hotspots or areas with high potential for conflict. Political management must be able to quickly identify where action is needed and respond accordingly in order to prevent major damage or defuse conflicts. And it must be constantly evaluated. It requires not only rapid response, but also continuous adaptation and constant evaluation of the decisions taken. A proactive, flexible and transparent approach is the key to defuse conflicts and prevent greater damage.

7. NOTES FOR PRACTICE

What happens on the international stage when a newly forged alliance rejects theoretically the initially formulated hopes? If a newly forged alliance on the international stage fails to meet theoretically formulated hopes, this means that the goals and expectations originally set are not fulfilled. In practice, the alliance therefore has difficulties realizing its goals. This has several serious consequences, both at political and global level.

Alliances are primarily formed to secure a certain strategic position of power, be it in the economic, security or diplomatic sphere. If this strategic position is not achieved due to the failure of the alliance, the states involved would face massive geopolitical disadvantages. A failed alliance would fall behind in areas such as trade, security issues or technology development and thus lose global competitiveness. Countries that had hoped for the success of the alliance could try to pursue their interests elsewhere, which would definitely destroy the regional balance of power. We witnessed this almost in disbelief during the escapades of the US Trump administration in early 2025.

Inevitably, new rivalries will emerge as other states or blocs attempt to fill the gap left by the failure of the alliance The shift in the balance of power would be threatening. In such cases, the actors involved must react quickly to either reinvigorate the alliance, rectify the mistakes or otherwise reorient themselves in order to safeguard their interests and global influence. The geopolitical arena is an ever-changing playing field where every mistake or setback creates a wave of new rivalries and power shifts. When countries that once banked on the success of an alliance suddenly feel that their hopes have come to nothing, the international deck of cards is quickly reshuffled. The dynamics of the crash are unpredictable, and while the members of the failed alliance are spinning in circles, power blocs may rejoice and use the opportunity to assert their own interests. Suddenly the world power struggle comes to the fore again and the original goal of cooperation, be it economic, security or scientific, seems like a distant dream. In this chaos, the attempt to fill the gap is more reminiscent of a competition than a diplomatic mission, whereby the seriousness of the situation seems almost humorous due to the maneuvering of the players.

The shift in the balance of power is becoming a dangerous game. Who will fill the vacuum? Who will emerge victorious from the situation? It is almost reminiscent of a battle for inheritance after a sudden chaotic change in leadership, with each new player emerging with their own ideas of order and prosperity, and this can be quite threatening in a world characterized by uncertainty.

For the players who now find themselves forced to react, it becomes an early spring-cleaning exercise in which they either try to regain trust by somehow reviving the failed alliance or simply have to reorient themselves elsewhere. The question remains as to who will pay the price for this geopolitical rollercoaster ride. Perhaps a little more foresight in the next alliances would not be the worst idea.

The geopolitical reality of 2025 was indeed characterized by unprecedented discord. In particular, peace efforts offered little incentive for the great madmen in Moscow who call the shots. For their chance of power lies in staging their brutality as a kind of instrument of power. In the context of war, maintaining power and influence is perceived as more important than finding a solution to the existing conflicts. In this perspective, peace negotiations or a ceasefire would be interpreted as weakness. The political logic in this case is therefore: the war must continue, even if it continues to destroy its own people and the international community.

The lack of any pressure on Moscow to enter into peace negotiations showed the perfidious reality. Power and face are then the only true currencies for those who hold the reins. The reality for the decision-makers in Moscow was less about the humanitarian impact of the war and more about political survival by continuing the war. Essentially, the war was viewed as a means to suppress internal unrest, stir up nationalism and distract from other internal problems.

For decision-makers in Moscow it's not just about the material goals of the war, but above all about political power, maintaining their presence in the eyes of the world and the survival of the regime. The lack of serious international pressure on Russia to engage in peace negotiations and the pursuit of power on the international stage demonstrate how deeply rooted the principles of power politics are and how difficult it is to resolve such conflicts through diplomatic means.

In this view, the outside world with its demands for

peace and negotiations hardly plays a role, as these take the form of an unmistakable threat to Moscow's internal power apparatus. The war mode becomes an instrument of self-assertion and international efforts to stop this course seem to be a losing game if they are not linked to real power and consequences. It is a dilemma that also poses massive challenges for the international community: how to deal with an actor that only sees its political existence legitimized through war, brutality and the preservation of power?

This mindset is particularly dangerous because it ignores the humanitarian costs of war and the long-term geopolitical consequences for the country and its population. The selfishness behind this logic leads to increased risk for its own citizens and destabilizes the international order by undermining the global consensus on the value of peace. The lack of willingness for peace leaves the international community helpless, especially since the remaining dictatorships want to profit from it.

The other madman on the other side of the Atlantic is not just profiting from this for himself and his followers. He is mixing a very special kind of poisonous mixture for the global unrest. It is amazing how some irrational political leaders, who are characterized by a populist, authoritarian world view, use uncertainty and division to secure their own power. In doing so, they are not only endangering their own country, but also the global order.

They increasingly see globality and the idea of a united peace as a threat. This creates a dangerous atmosphere in which multilateral cooperation is seen as a weakness and isolationism as a strength. Such behavior does not create stable solutions, but gnaws away at the foundations of a peaceful and cooperative world order. If this toxic cocktail is not defused, the global community is in danger of suffocating in a paternalism of the strongest, in which negotiations become a waste of time. Autocrats around the world, not only in North Korea or Iran, but also in Hungary or Turkey, seeing the success of such models, could try to adopt similar tactical moves, thereby further destabilizing global peace. Unfortunately, playing with such toxic tactics only leads to a cyclone of revenge, isolationism and insecurity in which the global community keeps lurching from one crisis to the next.

The challenge for the international community is enormous. How to deal with such a divisive, egotistical leadership? How to prevent this political stance from becoming the new norm? It is a question for the future that confronts world politics with the task of creating real consequences for such behavior, so that not only world leaders but also their followers learn that global cooperation and peace are not against their own interests, but are the key to a secure and prosperous future.

Dealing with divisive, self-serving leadership is daunting, but not insurmountable. Through international accountability, multilateral diplomacy, and fostering a culture of cooperation, the international community can counter the dangerous normalization of such leadership. The ultimate goal is to create a world in which global cooperation and peace are seen as the primary drivers of prosperity and security, benefiting not only nations but also the well-being of future generations. This requires concerted efforts by politicians, institutions, and individuals alike to transform the norms and values that govern global politics.

A central aspect of preventing divisive political attitudes from becoming the norm is a clear and determined response by the international community. When countries agree on common values, such as human rights, freedom, mutual respect and cooperation, they must also be willing to defend these values, even if it becomes uncomfortable or difficult. The international community, when united in its commitment to core values, can send a powerful message. This unified approach should not be dependent on the convenience or comfort of specific nations or leaders, but rather on the principle that these values are non-negotiable.

In global politics, the desire to avoid confrontation or the discomfort of taking a difficult stance often leads to inaction. However, as you point out, this is where the international community must show that there is no room for ambiguity when it comes to defending fundamental values. Inaction or weak responses allow oppressive regimes to perceive that their behavior can be tolerated, ultimately paving the way for the spread of divisive and harmful ideologies. There must be a consistent, coherent and unified voice when it comes to defending universal human rights, freedom, and democracy. If authoritarian leaders are not called out for their actions, it signals a lack of commitment to these principles. The international community must show that such behavior will not be tolerated. Leadership is not just about statements but about ensuring that policy, diplomacy, and action across all levels of governance reflect these values. From grassroots activism to international summits, there must be a cohesive effort to ensure that values are consistently defended and upheld.

When the international community stands united in its commitment to core values, this collective approach can send a strong message. The idea is not necessarily to use military force, but to maintain a credible threat of force, which can help prevent aggression without actual violence. However, deterrence must be complemented by other political and economic measures, not just military strength.

Deterrence alone is often not enough. When authoritarian regimes can be deterred not just through military force, but also through political and economic pressure, this is often the smarter and more sustainable approach. Relying solely on military deterrence might lead to, at worst, a hot war. Deterrence and military threats can be justified as short-term measures, but the ultimate aim must always be the promotion of a stable, just world order.

The world needs a renewed commitment to multilateral action in which states question their sovereignty in favor of common global interests. Countries should maintain and further develop cooperation platforms that enable them to overcome common economic, political and security challenges. Multilateralism, the principle that multiple states work together to address global problems, is essential in times of growing global uncertainty. It's not just about pooling resources, but also about sharing responsibility, knowledge and innovation. Challenges such as terrorism, cyberattacks, and nuclear proliferation require joint efforts. All nations must collaborate to ensure that threats are tackled across borders.

In the past, sovereignty was often seen as inviolable, but in a globalized world, solving the biggest challenges often requires a reconsideration of national interests within the framework of greater global welfare. Nations must understand that cooperation does not mean the loss of sovereignty, but rather that it's possible to protect national interests while taking on global responsibilities. This means aligning national policies with a shared international framework that addresses global issues. To tackle today's diverse challenges, nations need to maintain and develop cooperation platforms that allow for a structured exchange of ideas, resources and responsibilities.

The reality is that no country can solve the challenges of the 21st century alone. Multilateralism is not just about addressing common challenges but about taking global responsibility and securing the future of the next generations. This is especially critical in an era when nationalistic tendencies are rising, and the global community is increasingly at risk of fragmentation.The world needs more than just political and economic cooperation, it needs a global solidarity that prioritizes ethical principles and the desire for a better world. Only through such values can we ensure that cooperation remains sustainable and just. In this new era of global interconnectedness, nations must be ready to take responsibility for their actions in the international arena. This means they must feel committed not just to their own interests but also to the interests of the global community.

Social media and globalized communication should move quickly in the other direction. They can be used as a platform to promote positive, cooperative visions and to sensitize the public to the risks of a politics of hate and division. In many countries where authoritarian and nationalist forces are on the rise, there is an urgent need for young generations to develop a different vision of international cooperation. Programs that highlight intercultural exchange, international friendships and global responsibility can help to counteract the divisive forces that political leaders bring to society in the long term.

The question of how the international community deals with a divisive and selfish leadership is complex, but not unsolvable. A determined coalition of states, international organizations, civil society and the media is needed to put the value of global cooperation back at the heart of international politics. Only a global response can prevent authoritarian and isolationist attitudes from becoming a permanent norm. It is an uncomfortable, perhaps even adventurous path, but with common strategies these challenges can be overcome.

The answer to all the complex geopolitical challenges might even be simple, almost too simple. Probably sitting somewhere in a crowded conference room 17 diplomats who are brooding about the global peace plan and wondering why no one has ever come up with the obvious solutions. Maybe this is the way history has always told us to just do what we have to do. After all, what can go wrong?

8. EUROPE'S ANSWERS

Europe must be able to give answers, not only to its allies but also to those who want to destroy everything. Europe is not masochistic. It must show a clear, coherent stance that signals to all allies and opponents that it is ready to stand up for its interests and security. This requires a strategic approach that includes diplomacy, economic measures and, if necessary, military options. If Europe does not do this, one might imagine that it could end up as the global political equivalent of a bad neighbor who is always hiding behind closed doors while his front door is constantly being kicked in. Maybe it's time to not only swing the compass in a desired context, but also give it some momentum so that it points in the direction of a determined, clear and strategic response.

The path forward requires bold leadership, the political will to make tough decisions, and a sense of urgency. Europe must take proactive steps, such as investing in defense capabilities, technological innovation, and a sustainable economy, all while maintaining its commitment to democratic values and human rights. The challenges are immense, but the opportunities for Europe to play a transformative, leadership role on the global stage are equally great. By acting with urgency, determination, and vision, Europe can position itself as a strong and proactive global hub for the future.

Building temporary bridges, even if they are just pontoons, is always better than being frightened or even helpless to withdraw. It's not about building the perfect, massive bridge right away, but rather about focusing on the essentials. Acting, even if it is only a first step. Time is the crucial factor when it comes to achieving the breakthrough of decisive thinking and action. Because in a world that is changing at a rapid pace, no time can be wasted. The moment when Europeans make the right connections and build the first bridges could be the crucial one. In a world where change is happening at lightning speed, decisive action, no matter how small it seems, is often the key to unlocking larger breakthroughs.

Often, the first step toward addressing a complex global issue is the most important. Europe does not need to wait for perfect solutions or grand-scale plans before acting. Small initiatives, like coalitions of willing countries, cross-border collaborations, or localized efforts, can set the foundation for larger, more ambitious projects. Europe cannot afford to be passive or overly cautious. Speed in decision-making and action is critical. The world moves quickly, and by the time Europe hesitates, opportunities can be lost or worse, gaps can widen, allowing other powers such as China or Russia to fill them. Europe's window of opportunity for taking the lead on global challenges is limited.

Perfection is not the goal, pragmatic action is. Sometimes, temporary solutions can lead to permanent ones as they help establish relationships, understanding, and trust that are needed for more significant action later. Pontoons, not steel bridges, can often be the perfect place to begin.

The gaps that are opening up at global level and in political processes can be filled in the short term. However, this requires quick, targeted action that is simultanuously pragmatic and flexible. Rapid action, coupled with the willingness to enter into strategic alliances, can make the difference. However, if you forge alliances pro-actively, you will not only gain time but also secure resources and influence.

For its own political family, Europe is not a foreign body, but rather a living force nourished by the fundamental common roots. Europe is not just a geographical concept or a bureaucratic structure, it is the common foundation of values, ideals and historical experiences that have grown over centuries. These roots are deep and connect the peoples on a cultural, social and political level that goes far beyond national borders. It is precisely for this reason that the united peoples of Europe must not be indifferent to what happens with Ukraine, possibly with the Baltic countries or Poland. This unified force is not only an abstract concept, but should in practice form the basis for active and coherent action.

Global power shifts, political realignments, and economic instability have created new opportunities and challenges that require immediate attention. These gaps, while temporary, can quickly become permanent if not addressed in time. Forming strategic partnerships is one of the most powerful tools in Europe's arsenal for navigating current global gaps. By engaging in collaborative efforts, the different regions in congruence with the big body can gain resources, influence, and leverage that would otherwise be unavailable.

Europe must continue to pursue trade agreements and economic pacts with emerging economies and developing markets, thereby securing access to resources and markets that are crucial for its long-term stability.These partnerships should be focused on reciprocal benefits that align with Europe's long-term strategic goals.

Furthermore, Europe must ensure that its defense strategy is flexible, coherent, and cooperative to protect its interests and effectively navigate the increasingly complex global landscape. Its defense strategy must evolve to meet the challenges of both traditional and emerging threats. A flexible, coherent, and collaborative defense framework will be essential for ensuring security, stability, and strategic influence within and beyond Europe's borders.

The security environment is becoming more unpredictable, with challenges ranging from cybersecurity threats to hybrid warfare and unconventional conflicts. A flexible defense strategy allows Europe to pivot when necessary and adjust its responses to address new, evolving threats. There's Europe's perennial favorite, the "don't make waves" approach. This strategy has been known for decades, famous for saying, "let's just keep our heads down and hope that the problems of the world don't land in our backyard."

Europe's defense strategy must not resemble a well-organized, somewhat dated antique shop, full of shiny things, very pleasing to the eye, but completely unprepared for the challenges of today. When the wolves are at the door, Europe's defense policy may be too busy trying to curry favor with its neighbors to actually do anything about it. Will Europe remain stuck behind a door with a politely written "Do not disturb" sign, hoping that it will not be kicked in?

If Europe ignores the geopolitical challenges, it is not only playing with the fire in its own neighbourhood, but also questioning the very foundations of its own existence. For its allies, Europe is far more than just a nice neighbour who occasionally takes out the garbage cans; it is the strategic core that gives stability and direction. But if Europe fails to assume this responsibility, the whole structure of an alliance will collapse like a house of cards, only to be served as a willing snack by the dark powers of the globe. For those who do not act risk ending up in history as the continental procrastinator, who has lost his own relevance to the next geopolitical crisis.

It can be argued that the authoritarian tendencies in American society have both historical roots and current expressions, reinforced by social, economic and cultural factors. The Trump era has made these dynamics visible and reignited the debate about the future of democracy in the United States. The sociological view leads to a critical examination of various social, political and cultural aspects of the USA that are perceived as problematic in certain contexts. This statement is of course a very judgmental and critical expression that can be interpreted differently depending on perspective and ideological orientation. Nevertheless, lack of cohesive cultural depth or continuity.

The behavior of the US government and the often perceived aggressive and dominant global influence of the US have led to the alienation of many states from Western powers, with the US in particular often identified as the main actor in these geopolitical tensions. This behavior, observed at various historical stages, not only influenced the US's domestic political relations but also transformed its international relations with other states and regions.

Surprisingly, American President Donald Trump has ushered in an era of economic rethinking.With his policies, which were based on extensive deregulation, he has thoroughly confused the western economic culture, which for a long time relied on the principles of fiscal discipline and avoidance of over-indebtedness. Trump challenged the classic economic model, which was based on long-term stability and sustainable debt. Instead, he relied on short-term growth pushes through massive borrowing, which was seen by many as a departure from the conservative economic policies that were once considered to be a stable course.

Juggling protective tariffs is one of the most striking examples of Trump's economic blunders. In the end he scored a decent own goal. Because what he sold as fair trade practices leads to a global trade war that not only harms the US economy, but also hard hits its own consumers in the USA by higher prices on imported goods. And as he tries to shine in his America-first rhetoric, it quickly becomes clear that the long-term cost of these protective tariffs is not only in the form of higher prices for the American consumer, but also due to disrupted supply chains and a decline in international trade. Not to mention that US companies, which depend on global markets, suffer from trade barriers.

By practising the America First policy to the extreme, Trump is putting existing alliances at risk and driving a U-turn in Western foreign policy that is perceived by his allies as partly unpredictable, partly dangerous. From unilaterally withdrawing from international agreements such as the Paris climate accord to trade disputes with traditional partners, it has all been a reckless tactic that has eroded the ground of international standing. Trump's immeasurable misstep in canceling support for Ukraine in the face of Russia's brutal incursion into the country was not only politically disastrous, but morally reprehensible. By refusing to support Ukraine's legitimate resistance to Russia's aggression, he not only trampled on Western principles of freedom and democracy, but acted in a way that directly contributed to the suffering of millions of people. Even more serious is the fact that Trump, based on his personal preferences and a deeply flawed assessment of the geopolitical situation, even failed to pass on intelligence information available through satellite reconnaissance to Ukraine.

This negligent decision gave Russia carte blanche to bomb Ukraine without restraint. Carpets of bombs dropped on civilian targets turned the country into a field of rubble, reducing entire cities to ashes. This is not an isolated incident, but an ongoing attempt not only to dehumanize the Ukrainian people, but to systematically destroy them. And Trump, who actively encourages this assault, indirectly became part of this cruel plan. It was as if he opened the door to the mass murder of the Ukrainian people, to what must be considered a massive genocide, and supported the aggressor Russia in every possible way.

The extent of these acts cannot be downplayed.The decision to withhold intelligence and thus reduce Ukraine's ability to defend itself was more than just a grave mistake, it was active complicity. This failure had real, bloody consequences and makes Trump indirectly complicit in the barbaric war crimes perpetrated by Russia.

The USA, which once seemed to be based on principles such as respect for human rights, democracy and international law, suddenly found itself in a dangerous, unrestrained era under Trump's regime. American foreign policy, once a driving force behind global peace initiatives, has become under him a cynical playground where geopolitical power and selfish interests have been put before the lives of millions. The decision to abandon Ukraine was not only a geopolitical disaster, but also a moral low for the US.

The old legal principle "stupidity does not protect against punishment" remains. At some point, in the near or far future, there will be a moment when the actions of Trump and his clique must be tried before an international court. International tribunals should be able to punish such politically motivated crimes. For those who enrich themselves with the suffering of others and allow war crimes, must not hide behind the veil of ignorance or stupidity. There is no excuse for what Trump has done on the international battlefield, and eventually international law, even years or decades later, will be accountable.

What does political trust mean? Not only how can it be defined conceptually, but which factors determine it?

Political trust is complex. It includes confidence in the integrity and ability of politicians to act, as well as in the fairness and efficiency of political processes and institutions. Political trust is a fundamental component of the stability of a democracy, as it promotes acceptance of political decisions and willingness to participate in social processes.

However, political trust is not static, it evolves over time and is influenced by a wide range of factors. These include the performance of political leaders, the transparency and fairness of political institutions, economic conditions, social trust, and external factors such as global crises or political scandals. As circumstances change, so does public confidence in political institutions and actors.

These factors need to be continuously examined and evaluated, as they are constantly changing and changing due to new events and developments. A precise analysis of the causes and effects as well as an objective assessment of the political actors are therefore essential to optimise policy strategies and make the right decisions.

Political action is basically what has to be done to solve social problems, or at least to make them look that way. Sometimes it is about satisfying social needs, sometimes it is about the pursuit of power or the pursuit of one's own ideology. And, of course, public opinion plays a major role. The effects of these actions are usually just as complex as the causes. They range from changes in society to economic effects and geopolitical upheavals. When things go well, it strengthens confidence in the government. When things go wrong, the political scandals and disappointments come tumbling down. Ultimately, it is a mixture of competence, leadership and negotiating skills that determines whether political action is approved or not. It is therefore as if international politics were a constant balancing act.

If the European Union's decision-making capacity is

seriously undermined, the consequences are not only worrying but potentially catastrophic. Europe is at a crucial juncture where internal divisions, bureaucratic hurdles and a weakening of the common vision could jeopardize the basis for a stable and viable Union. It is no secret that the EU has repeatedly struggled with internal conflicts and a lack of unity in recent years. If these tendencies continue to grow, Europe could paralyze itself and lose its ability to respond to pressing global challenges. A Europe paralyzed by bureaucratic blockages or permanent disunity will quickly become irrelevant. It would be a Europe that loses its ability to be taken seriously as a global player.

Instead of influencing the international stage, it would become an easily vulnerable target for other geopolitical actors waiting to exploit the weakened remnants of the union and strengthen themselves. The scenario of a fragmented Europe, embroiled in internal conflicts and losing its collective capacity to act, would be a strategic disaster. Europe could end up in a position where it is unable to respond effectively to critical issues of global security, climate change, economic challenges or migration. In such a case not only the Europeans themselves would suffer, but also the world order as a whole could be destabilized.

Without a clear and coherent European response to global challenges, the geopolitical actors who are already lurking with interest in the EU's weaknesses would be able to advance their own agendas at the expense of Europe. Imagine that Europe would paralyse itself, be it through internal disputes, excessive bureaucracy or a weakening of the common vision, with disastrous consequences. A fragmented Europe that is unable to respond to global challenges will be a food for thought for geopolitical actors who are just waiting to absorb the leftovers.

It is therefore crucial that Europe strengthens its internal unity while at the same time optimising its ability to take decisions quickly and efficiently. The European Union must not sink into political paralysis, because geopolitical developments are moving at a rapid pace and Europe must be able to react decisively and with the ability to act. This would not only benefit the Union itself, but also global stability and security.

It has become both a duty and a responsibility for Europe. its institutions, its political actors, and above all its people, to protect and preserve its sovereignty. This requires a continuous and conscious effort to nurture and uphold its remarkable identity. Europe must never abandon what makes it unique. By embracing its own inherent strength, Europe lays the foundation to pursue future-oriented alliances on a grand scale. Only a confident, self-assured Europe can engage the world as a true partner, neither retreating into itself nor losing sight of its values.

It is inevitable that the free world will have to engage in a confrontation with the inhuman dictatorship of the Kremlin, the dangerous backstage maneuverings of

China and the and the massive cowboy-style cultural decline seen in parts of the United States History will show how this could be overcome, especially as the other terrorist attacks around the world are not diminishing. A guesswork approach will not be able to predict the outcome. Only efforts in security policy, research and business will be able to ensure that we do not slip up on the steps to the future.

Another pressing question within this context concerns the potential establishment of a nuclear shield, possibly even on the territory of the Baltic states. As geopolitical tensions rise and deterrence once again becomes a central theme in international relations, the deployment of such defense systems is no longer a theoretical discussion but a strategic imperative.

The mere consideration of a nuclear shield in Eastern Europe underscores the shifting security dynamics on the continent. It signals not only a response to the growing threat from the Kremlin's aggressive posture but also a recalibration of NATO's defense perimeter. For the Baltic nations, on the frontline of this confrontation, it would represent a powerful deterrent and a deeply symbolic assertion of sovereignty and alliance solidarity.

When Ukraine gave up the hardware of the nuclear system in the 1990s, where did the software leave the knowledge? When Ukraine gave up the hardware, that is to say the bombs and missiles, another crucial component remained on the way, knowledge. And when Russia later began to flinch the security guarantees, it quickly turned out that Ukraine without its nuclear shield became an easy target.

One central point is the need for a comprehensive understanding and solid infrastructure for nuclear safety. The management and control of nuclear weapons requires not only technical knowledge, but also strict political and military discipline. Ukraine's experience shows how fragile security arrangements can be, and highlights the importance of stable and reliable systems for conflict prevention.

Even if the worst-case scenario does not necessarily occur, it is crucial to prepare for it with a clear vision, strong unity and an unwavering will to preserve and develop the European idea. But this must also be made clear to the public, every single citizen. It is not enough for policymakers to act internally and cook their own soup. Everyone should consider why a strong and capable Union is more necessary than ever, and above all why everyone is part of this process.

It is about making people aware that the challenges facing Europe are not abstract, but have a direct impact on their daily lives. Economic instability, political polarization or security threats affect the entire population. How Europe responds to these challenges will determine the future of generations to come. When the peoples of Europe recognise that the cohesion and ability to act of the Union is not only a political or economic objective, but directly affects their personal quality of life and security, will also increase the willingness to support these processes.

Political communication plays a crucial role in this. It must be clear and transparent why Europe makes decisions, which steps are necessary and why sometimes difficult but necessary measures are needed to strengthen the Union. The dialogue with citizens must take place on an equal footing, their concerns and concerns must be taken seriously, while at the same time promoting understanding of the long-term benefits of a united and capable Europe.

Another aspect is the emotional component. It is not only about facts and data, but also about the feeling of belonging and common commitment. The European idea must go from a political vision to a real, tangible goal for which everyone is committed. This is the only way to ensure that Europe as a pan-European community emerges stronger from crises, while maintaining the solidarity and trust of the population.

Ultimately, the message must be clear that Europe is not a distant institution but a project that matters to all. The responsibility to shape and secure it lies in the hands of each individual citizen. Only together, with a strong united Europe, can we meet the global challenges and preserve the level of prosperity as well as security for future generations.

9. WHAT DOES EUROPE THINK OF ITSELF?

The question What does Europe think about this? is profound because it requires not only a political or ethical response, but also a reflection on the identity of Europe as a whole. What makes it special? How is its identity composed? Who is Europe really? Who defines it and who are its bearers?

Europe as a geopolitical construct and idea is much more than the institutions in Brussels or Strasbourg. It is a continent that has evolved over centuries, with a deep-rooted history ranging from the ancient Greeks and Romans to the political and social upheavals of the last two centuries. Nevertheless, Europe is not only defined by political elites, but also by European society as a whole, which is composed of different actors.

In a classical political sense, Europe could be seen as the Union or as the totality of European countries. But the

European public is much more than that. How great is the influence of this broad European public on what is understood as European opinion or European thinking? European society is a colourful mix that extends across different social, cultural and political strata. It is shaped not only by the intelligentsia or political elites, but also by the broad sections of the population: workers, entrepreneurs, students, artists and above all the middle class, which must not be missing, how Europe is integrated into people's everyday lives.

In reality Europe's political leadership is often shaped by a certain elite, the policy-makers, diplomats, experts and academics who make the complex decisions about the future of the Union. This intelligentsia has the last word in many ways, but its decisions must also be supported by the general population, whether through elections, referendums or general public opinion.

Is the intelligentsia of Europe really ideally part of the bourgeoisie? This is an exciting question, because in the classical sense, the middle class is often understood as the middle class, those who are characterized by economic stability, education and social responsibility. Intelligentia, on the other hand, includes the academic and intellectual elite, scientists, philosophers, historians and political thinkers whose perspective is often shaped by theoretical reflection.

In an ideally constructed Europe, where all social groups are actively involved in shaping their future, one could argue that these two groups should not be separated but rather united. At best, intelligentsia and bourgeoisie are closer than one might think. Both act as a kind of symbiosis in an evolving society, sharing practical knowledge and philosophical and political reflection. A society in which intellect and practical way of life are in balanced dialogue could be considered as future-proof and resilient. But in reality, there are often tensions between these groups, a divide that is reinforced by growing alienation and mistrust of the political elite.

Beyond the political or ethical taste, Europe presents itself as a construct torn between idealism and realpolitik. The political elite often has a different agenda than the broad classes. Important policy decisions, such as the EU's role in global conflicts or migration, have a massive impact on the daily lives of all citizens, but not always in a way that is directly consistent with their own needs or values. Europe as an institution often seems to move in a balance between the demands of institutions and the real needs of people, which can not hide a sense of alienation.

The task for Europeans is to bridge the gap between levels and create a collective identity shared by all parts of society. Europe is not just a bureaucracy or a market, but a community of people with different experiences and perspectives who must share a common future.

The question of how to get a grip on the political criminals, those who do not cooperate constructively but block progress through obstructive or malicious behavior before they trigger a catastrophe will be decisive. It is not only about corruption or illegitimate interests, but also the question of how to create a political culture that brings together cooperation, responsibility and ethical behavior instead of tolerating destructive behavior.

Mechanisms for transparency and accountability in politics should be established, enabling the public and control institutions to identify and act on misconduct. Another important step is the promotion of a political culture based on cooperation, consensus and responsibility. When the political discourse is dominated by negativism, agitation and obstruction, politics loses credibility and is perceived as self-referential. To change this culture, political actors, the media and the public must work for constructive solutions. This means that on the political stage more value must be placed on finding solutions rather than merely naming and shedding problems.

The voters must make a conscious choice for those decision-makers who take their responsibility seriously, instead of giving their vote to those who only sabotage the political operation. However, this requires an informed and engaged electorate that understands that political blockades and destructive behaviour threaten their own standard of living and social stability in the long run.

Mechanisms for transparency and accountability in politics should be established, enabling the public and control institutions to identify and act on misconduct. Another important step is the promotion of a political culture based on cooperation, consensus and responsibility. When the political discourse is dominated by negativism, agitation and obstruction, politics loses credibility and is perceived as self-referential. To change this culture, political actors, the media and the public must work for constructive solutions. This means that on the political stage more value must be placed on finding solutions rather than merely naming and shedding problems.

Another important step is to promote public discourse in which political misconduct is exposed and questioned. The media and journalists play a key role in this. Investigative journalism and public debate are necessary to draw attention to political misconduct and blockades, and to expose those who act in a destructive way. A public well-informed by think tanks and evaluation agencies can act as a leverage to get politicians to rethink their tactics.

While reformist movements can lead to positive social and political change, destructive movements that reject institutions, norms, and scientific consensus can destabilize societies and lead to polarization and even violence. Reformist movements aim to address systemic issues within existing frameworks without attempting to completely dismantle institutions. They are often grounded in the belief that societal problems can be solved through changes to laws, policies, and practices.

These movements typically promote ideals like equality, justice, and human rights, and they work to make these ideals a reality through non-violent means. While reformist movements seek to create positive change through the modification of existing systems, destructive anti-establishment movements reject the legitimacy of those systems entirely. These movements are often driven by extreme discontent and frustration with the current state of affairs, but instead of seeking to improve or reform the system, they aim to dismantle or replace it. This can lead to several dangerous consequences.

One of the hallmarks of destructive movements is their attack on established institutions, such as the government, the judiciary, the media, and scientific bodies. By portraying these institutions as corrupt, illegitimate, or oppressive, they weaken public trust and undermine the social fabric of a society. The outcome is a society divided along lines of ideology, class, race or geography, where consens becomes nearly impossible.

Across Europe, right-wing populist movements have also benefited from anti-establishment sentiment, blaming immigrants, the European Union and global elites for the economic problems of ordinary citizens. The long-term consequences of destructive movements can be devastating. Societies that experience deep polarization and distrust in institutions face significant challenges in governance and social cohesion.

As institutions become discredited and fragmented, democracy itself can be undermined. In extreme cases, anti-establishment movements can lead to the erosion of democratic norms and the rise of authoritarian regimes. Prolonged periods of polarization and unrest can lead to social fragmentation, with different groups within society increasingly at odds. This creates an environment ripe for violence, extremism, and civil conflict. The Balkans in the 1990s is a tragic example of how nationalism, rejection of institutions, and anti-establishment rhetoric led to violent ethnic conflict and the disintegration of a region. Destructive anti-establishment movements aren't confined to any one nation, they can have ripple effects across borders, especially in an interconnected world. When one country experiences political instability due to these movements, it can influence neighboring countries, trade relationships, and global diplomatic efforts. The rise of populism and anti-globalization sentiment, for example, has caused significant shifts in international relations, such as Brexit and growing tensions between nations.

Combating destructive behaviour requires a multidimensional approach. It requires clear legal and institutional measures, ensuring transparency and accountability, promoting a constructive political culture and building a politically engaged and informed society. But the crucial step is to stress the importance of responsibility and cooperation in political work, and to remove those who are exclusively destructive from politics, be it through elections, political sanctions or public pressure. The crucial step, however, is to emphasize the importance of responsibility and cooperation in political work and to remove those who act exclusively destructively from politics, whether through elections, political sanctions, or public pressure. To mitigate the risks of destructive movements, societies must prioritize education, critical thinking and dialogue while ensuring that democratic institutions remain strong and resilient in the face of populist challenges. Only by strengthening trust in institutions and creating opportunities for constructive political engagement can we hope to counteract the destabilizing effects of extreme anti-establishment ideologies.

When democratic institutions lose their political effectiveness and populist movements thrive, societies face significant risks, risks that, if not effectively addressed, can lead to chaos. Europe, with its long and turbulent history of wars, revolutions, and totalitarian regimes, is particularly vulnerable to these destabilizing forces. If countries fail to prioritize education, critical thinking, and dialogue, the continent risks the collapse of the very democratic ideals it has fought so hard to preserve for centuries.

The rise of extreme anti-establishment ideologies has the potential to cause profound social fragmentation. If the political landscape becomes divided to the point where different groups view each other not as fellow citizens but as adversaries, it becomes incredibly difficult to maintain social cohesion. In such a scenario, cooperation becomes impossible. When people stop trusting institutions and each other, it opens the door for societal breakdown.

If Europe were to fall into a protectionist spiral, with countries retreating from trade agreements and isolationist policies taking hold, the economic ramifications could be severe. The European Union, which has historically been a cornerstone of peace and prosperity on the continent, could fracture. Trade disruptions, economic downturns, and job losses would only deepen existing inequalities, leading to further disillusionment with institutions and fueling more extremist ideologies.

The EU has always been more than just an economic union. It is a political project aimed at ensuring peace, stability and prosperity after the horrors of the world war. Protectionism would fundamentally undermine the EU's core mission, which is based on cooperation, integration and collective decision-making. Member states, many of whom already harbor Eurosceptic sentiments, might push for their own economic autonomy, leading to a potential unraveling of the Union. If countries begin to retreat into nationalism and economic isolation, the EU could face an existential crisis, with some members opting to leave or demanding a complete overhaul of its governing structure.

History has shown ideological differences breeds ideological differences and erroneous views often breeds extremism. A protectionist shift could embolden nationalist and far-right populist movements, which are already gaining ground across Europe. Politicians who decry the EU as a force of globalism, alienating national sovereignty, could use turmoil to further their anti-establishment narratives. If they succeed, it could lead to a rise in authoritarian policies, as these movements often promise strong leadership.

A Europe caught in a protectionist spiral would not only face internal fragmentation but also become increasingly irrelevant on the global stage. Historically, the EU has been an advocate for multilateralism, free trade and diplomacy, projecting its influence globally through partnerships and agreements with countries and regions around the world. Protectionism would undo this role.

If Europe turns inward, its ability to influence global trade and international relations would diminish. The EU has long been a key player in promoting human rights, climate change initiatives and diplomatic engagement worldwide. If it retreats behind its own borders, the vacuum could be filled by other powers, most notably

China and the United States. A more fragmented Europe would struggle to assert itself in the global arena, leading to diminished power and the erosion of its position as a global leader in trade and diplomacy.

Protectionism doesn't just affect intra-European trade, it also leads to strained relations with non-EU countries. Countries in the Balkans, Eastern Europe, and North Africa, which rely on trade agreements with the EU, would feel the economic sting of a retreating Europe. The EU could face growing tensions with these regions, with economic disruptions leading to political instability or even migration crises as people seek better opportunities outside their home countries.

The consequences of a protectionist spiral would be devastating for both the European project and the broader global system. Without a united, integrated Europe, the continent could face economic collapse, political fragmentation, and social unrest. The threat of authoritarianism would grow, and extremist ideologies would thrive in the fertile soil of disillusionment and desperation. The fragmentation of the EU, which has historically been a symbol of peace and prosperity, would not only undermine European stability but also risk plunging the world into another period of geopolitical uncertainty.

This is not a trivial matter. The rise of protectionism, far from being a cynical or detached concern, is a real and present threat that could push Europe into chaos. If Europe's leaders fail to prioritize cooperation, dialogue and open engagement, the continent risks becoming a battleground for competing nationalist ideologies, with dire consequences for democracy, peace, and global stability. Europe must now ask itself whether it will reaffirm its commitment to unity and international cooperation or allow fear, isolationism, and populism to fracture the very fabric of its society. The choice is one of immense consequence, not only for Europe but for the world as a whole.

10. DEFENSE READINESS

The advance in international cooperation consists of a credible willingness to act effectively. Credibility comes from concrete, actionable steps that show that a country or organization is actually willing to take responsibility and help solve common problems. It is not enough to make declarations of intent; the international community expects commitments to be translated into action. Whether it is peacekeeping, climate protection or the fight against poverty, action must be effective and sustainable. Otherwise, the credibility of a country or institution in cooperation is quickly undermined.

In many cases, the willingness to defend oneself is the key factor for gaining and securing the trust of other countries. A country that takes its own security and that of its allies seriously signals not only the ability to protect itself, but also the willingness to act as a reliable partner in crisis situations.

A crucial element for meaningful progress in international relations is credibility coupled with action. Mere promises or the signing of agreements are not enough. True progress in cooperation between nations relies on a genuine and credible commitment to practical and effective steps toward achieving common goals. For international cooperation to progress, countries must not only express good intentions but also back them up with concrete, coordinated actions with tangible results. The emphasis here is on trust, accountability, and consistent implementation. Without a willingness to act, or the credibility of that willingness, cooperation remains more theory than practice. All of this can be precisely verified and measured. It just requires the necessary external tools. However, for cooperation to be truly meaningful, one fundamental principle must underpin all efforts, a credible willingness to act effectively.

Declarations of intent are not uncommon on the international stage. Summits, treaties, and resolutions often produce impressive statements about shared goals and values. However, without concrete, sustained and measurable action, these words risk becoming hollow. Effective international cooperation is not measured by how many speeches are given or agreements are signed, but by how well those agreements are implemented and how consistently partners honor their commitments. To preserve credibility, action must not only be visible but also sustainable and impactful. Short-term political gains should not take precedence over long-term global stability. In areas like poverty reduction or peacekeeping, success depends on strategies that are inclusive, locally adapted and resilient to setbacks. Mutual trust is paramount, as collective security depends on the unwavering support of all members. A reluctance to act when one ally is under threat not only weakens the alliance but also emboldens adversaries.

Joint defense requires a shared mindset, a readiness to act decisively and in unison. That means investing in military readiness, coordinating strategies and showing political will even in difficult circumstances. An alliance in which members doubt each other's resolve is an alliance at risk.To strengthen international cooperation, nations and organizations must embrace a culture of accountability, transparency, and results-oriented action. This involves setting realistic but ambitious goals, regularly monitoring progress and reporting, following through on commitments, even when domestic pressures make it difficult. The credibility of a country or an alliance is not built overnight, but through consistent, effective and sustainable action over time. In a world where cooperation is not a luxury but a necessity, credibility is not just a virtue, it is a strategic imperative.

Defence readiness is not limited to military strength. It also includes the ability to cooperate on international security issues, such as peacekeeping missions or combating transnational threats such as terrorism and cyber attacks. It is also a question of diplomatic, economic and strategic measures to ensure the security of the international community and its own security.

Diplomacy is a key mechanism for maintaining stable alliances, as it strengthens trust between partners.

In this context, it is crucial that the defence readiness is not understood as isolationism or unilateral aggression but as part of a collective security approach based on cooperation, trust and protection of common values. When a country uses its defence preparedness with the aim of stabilising the international order and preventing conflicts, it is perceived as a reliable partner in international cooperation.

A typical example where the system is being rigidly undermined is Trump's foreign policy. Trump's „America First" approach focuses exclusively on national interests and thus relies on isolationism and unilateral measures that undermine trust and cooperation with traditional allies. Examples of this are the withdrawal from international agreements such as the Paris climate agreement or the Iran nuclear agreement. These decisions led to a loss of credibility in the eyes of many countries, which were confident that the US would take its international obligations seriously.

The withdrawal from such agreements was recognized as unpredictable and a lack of willingness to cooperate on a global level. The international community concluded an agreement in 2015 to prevent Iran from becoming a nuclear power. The 2015 agreement was signed by the US, the five permanent members of the UN Security Council, Great Britain, France, Russia, China, the USA and Germany, and Iran. The aim was to prevent Iran from developing nuclear weapons by limiting its uranium enrichment to a low level and strengthening the international monitoring and inspection system of the International Atomic Energy Agency. In return, economic sanctions against Iran have been eased. Since Trump's withdrawal from this pact, Iran's uranium enrichment efforts have augmented dramatically and have come just short of nuclear weapons capability.

In this sense, the example shows how the withdrawal

from a multilateral agreement and the lack of a credible commitment to effective action accelerates the escalation of a geopolitical problem. International cooperation was undermined by Trump's decision, which not only damaged confidence in the US but also aggravated the global security situation.

Another example is Trump's NATO policy, in which he repeatedly questioned whether the US was still committed to supporting its allies as part of the defense alliance. This attitude not only damaged the credibility of the USA as a reliable partner, but also trust within NATO. Trump's foreign policy undermined defense readiness in the global context and affected confidence in the US's ability and willingness to cooperate and take responsibility on a global level. This has resulted in a sense of insecurity among many international partners.

Europe now faces the challenge of taking responsibility for its own security and the global order on the one hand and not falling into passive cowardice or cowering before power-obsessed geopolitical players such as Russia, China or the USA on the other. It is a difficult balance not to be intimidated or blackmailed by these forces. This means that Europe must be able to draw a clear line in relation to Russia, China and the US that includes the defense of its own interests and the safeguarding of universal values. This could be done through cooperation with partners such as Canada, Australia or Japan in order to form a common front against authoritarian tendencies worldwide.

An important point for Europe will be not to become too dependent on a single geopolitical actor, be it the US, Russia or China. Europe must develop a strategic independence that encompasses both military and economic dimensions. This means that Europe must invest in its own defense in the long term and must not be overly dependent on individual players in terms of technology, trade and energy supply.

This may sound like a contradiction, but in international

politics it is important to combine European values and pragmatic realpolitik. Europe must remain true to itself and at the same time react realistically and flexibly to changing geopolitical circumstances. It will not always be easy to find the right balance between moral integrity and the necessities of diplomacy. Appeasement diplomacy often overlooks the fact that trying to defuse conflicts through endless compromises or avoiding difficult talks is much more dangerous in the long term than drawing clear boundaries and taking a stand at an early stage. In international politics, the good intention to avoid conflict often has the unintended consequence of allowing tensions to build up and escalate at a later date.

Diplomatic restraint to keep the dove of peace is justified. But sometimes this strategy backfires. If you are careful not to get too close to the other country in order to save face or to avoid unnecessarily exacerbating the conflict, your opponent may interpret this restraint as weakness. You could almost say that the constant hesitation and evasion of controversial issues acts as a free pass that encourages the other party to continue provoking or to assert their own interests at the expense of their opponent.

A classic example was the Cold War, which had many years of diplomatic hesitation and cautious rapprochement, but also the feeling that one or other opponent could be won with gentleness. The problem arose that during this time strategic positions were solidified, conflicts postponed and differences hardened. Until suddenly, in the worst case scenario, the world could lurch into a hot war if we were unable to send clear messages in time.

It's not about threatening with a club in every situation, but about finding the right balance. Diplomacy can remain calm and respectful, but at the same time it must be assertive and clear in its communication. A "no" should be taken just as seriously as a 'yes', and a clear "not with us" can do more to secure peace than a vague "maybe someday". There is safety in clarity: no one is forced to guess or feel insecure.

It must not remain just lip service. In a cynical view, Europe, which no longer takes a clear stance in an increasingly multipolar world, would either become a political bystander or a pawn in the hands of the major powers. In such a scenario, the European idea of a union of values and cooperation could largely fade into the background and Europe would become a geopolitical minor player, no longer in a position to actively shape the world order. It is not just a question of finding the right words, but above all of backing up these words with concrete action. The international community has long since recognized that what matters most is action, not empty promises. If Europe merely persists with declarations of intent and fails to act consistently, it will quickly lose its credibility and influence. Europe must no longer rely solely on fine words and declarations of intent. It must have the courage and determination to back up its principles with concrete, often difficult, actions.

The EU summit in Brussels, which was held quickly at the beginning of 2025, still revealed a mixed picture in terms of the determination and unity of the member states. One notable point of contention was Hungary's refusal to condemn the Russian war of aggression against Ukraine. Prime Minister Viktor Orbán blocked a declaration to this effect, which undermined the EU's unity on this key issue.

Nevertheless, the 27 heads of government showed remarkable unity on the rearmament of Europe. Supported by EU Commission President Ursula von der Leyen, they decided to spend 650 billion euros on defense over the next four years and to set up an additional fund of 150 billion euros. These funds are intended to strengthen the EU's defense capabilities, reduce strategic dependencies and promote the European defense industry.

If the whole European "theater" turns out to be a slowly creeping chimera, something that is more illusion than reality, then that would probably be an even gloomier picture of the EU than what we are currently experiencing. Instead of a dynamic, unified community capable of responding decisively to global challenges, the EU could turn out to be a slow, hesitant and overly bureaucratic institution, bogged down in internal discussions and party political games even in the most urgent crises.

In this vision, the EU would appear more like a ghost community, lacking the necessary determination to respond to the really burning issues on the world stage. Its power and influence would increasingly go up in smoke, a chimera that exists in political discourse but has no real substance to effect concrete change. The EU would then not only have missed out on its idealistic principles of peace, stability and prosperity, but would have drowned in a sea of disunited member states and stalled reform processes. Instead of presenting the

European project as a shining example of cooperation and integration, the EU might turn out to be more caught up in its own importance and self-perception than in its ability to actually act.

One might wonder what would remain of such a chimera. Often a kind of bureaucratic apparatus-construct that insists on being bigger and more important, while at the same time in reality it is falling apart. And then it becomes an increasingly frustrating question for citizens. If Europe is not able to come together and act, where will the political force that breaks this chimera stay?

Perhaps the real lesson is that the EU needs to evolve further, away from sluggish bureaucracy and towards a more flexible, determined Union capable of acting rather than always suffocating in its own discussions. Otherwise, the play could actually turn into a farce and Europe would lose itself in an ever-deepening chimera. For the peoples of the continent, this would indeed bring with it a dramatic and painful chain of suffering. In a scenario where the Union fails to assume its responsibility for a stable, autonomous and value-based international order and instead becomes increasingly dependent on the outside, confidence in the European idea and institutions will be completely eroded. Ultimately, the people of Europe could be the real losers in this development, as they would suffer not only from geopolitical powerlessness but also from political and social consequences.

This could have devastating effects, especially for the economically weaker countries. They would be forced to bow to the economic interests of others, since the Union as a whole would not be able to contribute to a fair distribution of wealth and development within the continent. Instead of creating prosperity, the Union would act as a kind of instrument for economic oppression that increases the wealth of the powerful while the peoples themselves fall into poverty or insecurity.

In such a scenario, the peoples of Europe would experience chains of dependence, deprivation and humiliation. It would be the result of a Union that has lost its own ability to act and a policy that has failed to protect people and defend the European community of values. Instead of a continent playing an active role in shaping the global future, people would live in a world where their voices are barely heard and where their rights and security are increasingly determined by the interests of others.

Whether the peoples of Europe are aware of the full extent of their current geopolitical situation and the possible consequences of a failure of the European Union is a complex question. There is a wide range of awareness and political perception in Europe, which strongly depends on various factors, including education, political orientation, media consumption, and the respective national history and experience. In the more central member states such as Germany, France and the Netherlands there is often a greater awareness of the

137

EU's role as a global player. These countries are more integrated into the European Union economically and politically, and often see the EU as an instrument for representing their interests on a global level. In these countries, the awareness of the geopolitical importance of the EU and the need for a strong, unified foreign policy is more widely recognised.

In the eastern and southern member countries, perceptions are often more strongly influenced by recent history, such as the transition from authoritarian regimes to democracies. They value the EU as a safeguard against external threats and a guarantor of democratic stability. Here too, the awareness of the need for a strong EU may be very high from a geopolitical perspective, but there is a certain gap, especially in countries where national interests are considered more important than common European values.

In the smaller, less central EU countries, such as Ireland

or Greece, there is sometimes a differentiated image of Europe that is more focused on national interests. Here, awareness of the EU's geopolitical role can often be less pronounced, especially if the feeling of security and prosperity within the Union is seen as given. But even in these countries, there are growing concerns about the loss of sovereignty and the increasing dependence on unloved actors, especially as political and economic tensions increase.

In these contexts, the awareness of geopolitical uncertainty and the possible long-term consequences of a weak, incapacitated EU is sometimes seen as too abstract to play a major role in political discourse. Instead, the focus is often on immediate national interests without looking at the broader geopolitical implications. Populist parties use this discontent to paint the image of a union that harms people rather than protects them, distorting the perception of Europe's geopolitical influence.

Another important factor is that some EU citizens are not fully informed about the geopolitical implications of the current political situation. In some countries, there is little intense discussion about European foreign policy or the long-term risks of a politically weak union. Many people are preoccupied with everyday social challenges and do not feel that geopolitical issues play an immediate role in their lives. Political apathy and disinterest in the complex global situation are the result.

In addition, the influence of the media on the assessment of geopolitical issues is often limited. In many countries, media companies focus on national and short-term issues rather than the long-term geopolitical challenges facing Europe. This reinforces the ignorance or lack of clear awareness of the possible consequences of a weak and divided European Union.

On the other hand, there are a growing number of Europeans who recognize the geopolitical uncertainties and are increasingly worried about that Europe could lose its position as a community of values and sovereign actor in a world of authoritarian regimes and global tensions. These concerns are reinforced by events such as the war in Ukraine, the challenges of climate change or the increasing geopolitical power of China. Recent geopolitical developments in particular have enhanced awareness among many Europeans of the need for a united and capable Union.

So, it can be said that awareness of the geopolitical challenges facing Europe and its possible consequences is present in the population, but often to varying degrees and depending on the context. While some countries and populations clearly recognise the dangers, in other parts of Europe there is considerable ignorance or a tendency to neglect the long-term effects of current EU policies. Awareness of these risks could grow even further if Europe is not able to respond decisively to the growing global challenges.

When the gloomy scenarios, that is to say if Europe loses

its political ability to act, sink into economic dependence and drift the peoples in a sea of deprivation and humiliation, then the result could become a true master class in political tragicomedy. A story in which the continent of philosophers and thinkers becomes a curious, bureaucratic puppet theater in which the strings are drawn from Beijing, Moscow and Washington.

The social perception of security has changed. Do young people today really grow up in an intellectual environment that successfully pretends to be illusory worlds? These conditions can be the reason for questioning the importance of a robust defense. In addition, most left-leaning education systems do not adequately address the issue of security policy, which is responsible for the lack of understanding of the complexity of the actual situation. Young people are reluctant to engage with these issues without a sound knowledge of the role of defence and security in society.

The declining defence propensity among young

generations in Europe is a worrying phenomenon with profound social and political implications. Many young people no longer seem to regard the importance of security and defence as a priority. Many are terribly afraid of losing their job, getting under the inflation screw, not getting enough pension once to lose the vacation they deserve, but when it comes to protecting their bare lives from any attack, to defend their general goods of the energy supply, the transport structures of public institutions, they shrug. They do this because they don't want to see it as acute. They negligently push aside the reality, which should be above all secondary practices.

Ultimately, it will be important for society as a whole to recognise that security is a common concern of all citizens. Only through an active engagement with these issues will the generations be guided to take responsibility for their society. Instead of worrying about how to fight an aggressor, they are more concerned with the question of how to lead life optimally as an

Instagram influencer. But the idea that all this could be lost under the auspices of a military attack seems too far-fetched to seriously consider.

Is it really just the sad realization that society, in its belief of prosperity and comfort, sits on a pile of cardboard? The awareness of security is about as relevant as a dusty relic from the time when it was believed that war was impossible in this country. It seems to reassure the general opinion that there is certainly time for a last TikTok video when things get rough.

11. THE GAME OF THE AUTOCRATS

The supreme autocrat, perhaps the coldest and cruelest, rules the Kremlin today, the King of Untouchability, who regards the Kremlin as a personal castle in which he comfortably settles power and no one can show him the door so quickly. Putin has forced changes that allow him an unlimited term. Critics see this type of government as a sign of authoritarian rule, which leaves little room for political opposition. Under Putin's rule, independent media in Russia were suppressed, closed down and journalists banned. The Kremlin has been persecuting opposition voices and activists. Famous cases such as the murder of journalist Anna Politkovskaya or the arrest and killing of Alexei Navalny raise questions about freedom of the press and separation of powers.

Russia's military interventions in Georgia in 2008, and in Ukraine in 2014 and 2022 have initially aroused international mistrust and little countermeasures. The annexation of the Crimea and the military attack on Ukraine were considered by many countries as a violation of international law. Acts of sabotage, detected Russian traces on the seabed of the Baltic Sea, drones over military bases or energy terminals in Europe as well as huge expenditure on armaments indicate extensive warlike plans. The daily bombardment of Ukrainian civilians with targeted attacks on hospitals, schools, kindergartens with deliberate second waves of bombs to hit the emergency services does not indicate that the Kremlin is ready for peace negotiations. They are a strategic reality. These are tactics of terror and deliberate escalation, unmistakable in their message.

It is cynical and dishonest of Russian diplomats to dismiss the growing sense of urgency in Europe as a sentiment hysteria. Such statements aim to trivialize a response that is not only justified, but absolutely necessary given the growing evidence of hybrid warfare and conventional aggression. Calling Europe's response to this brutal reality "hysteria" is an attempt to manipulate public perception and weaken resolve. But the facts on the ground speak louder than diplomatic distractions. Peace cannot be negotiated with those who show no interest in dialogue, but only in domination. And credibility in international cooperation requires not naive hope, but the courage to react appropriately and decisively.

In the sidelines, there are numerous reports and evidence that Russia under Putin has interfered in the political processes of other countries. The Russian government is accused of having at least indirectly interfered in elections in western democracies through cyber attacks, disinformation and support for extreme political forces. Russia under Putin has repeatedly committed human rights violations against the Ukrainian civilian population, including child abduction, torture and murder. The persecution of opponents, the suppression of minorities and the aggressive foreign policy reinforced the scepticism towards Putin. Russia pursues a policy aimed at expanding its influence in former Soviet states and beyond, which is perceived as a threat by neighboring countries and western states, but is too weakly countered.

The potential threats posed by Vladimir Putin and the Russian government are indeed well known to all and play an important role in geopolitical perception and international relations. Putin has regularly emphazised his military strength, including the threat to use nuclear weapons. Russia, under Putin's leadership, has modernized its nuclear weapons and over the last few years has repeatedly threatened to develop new nuclear weapons such as hypersonic guided missiles and strategic nuclear weapons. In this way, Putin uses military and political influence in various regions of the world to secure his position of power. Examples are the support of authoritarian regimes in Syria, Venezuela or Belarus and the breeding of separatists in eastern Ukraine. These threat potentials create tensions and fears at the international level, as many countries, especially in the West, consider Russia's long-term strategy and intentions under Putin to be destabilizing and confrontational. The combination of military strength and political influence makes Russia an extremly dangerous player on the international stage.

US President Trump has also repeatedly undermined confidence in basic democratic institutions in the US. The concerns point to how his actions and relationships with autocratic leaders, like Vladimir Putin and Kim Jong-un, were often seen as contrary to the core values of democracy and human rights that the U.S. has traditionally championed. Critics argued that by emphasizing personal relationships over ideological alignment, Trump potentially weakened the U.S.'s standing as a promoter of democratic values. This approach was seen by many as a departure from previous U.S. presidents who sought to challenge authoritarian regimes and promote liberal democratic ideals.

On the domestic front, his repeated undermining of

democratic institutions, such as questioning the legitimacy of elections, attacking the press and weakening checks and balances, also contributed to concerns about the erosion of democratic norms within the U.S. These actions fueled debates over the state of democracy in the country and left many questioning the health of its institutions.One particularly striking example is his refusal to acknowledge the results of the 2020 presidential election and the false allegations of electoral fraud he spread. He instigated the "Assault on the Capitol" on January 6, 2021, in which his supporters tried to prevent election certification. Trump's attacks on the independence of the judiciary, as well as his attempts to influence investigations against his government or himself, has also shaken confidence in the rule of law.

During his presidency there were numerous accusations of corruption and conflicts of interest, for example in connection with his business and the influence that his family and group had on his political decisions. Trump is known for his lack of transparency and for withholding information, especially on important issues such as the response to the pandemic or in connection with secret information. His close relations with autocratic leaders such as Vladimir Putin, Kim Jong-un and others underscore how he is courting authoritarian regimes while ignoring the values of democracy and human rights, raising doubts about his stance on international standards and norms. One particularly striking example is his refusal to acknowledge the results of the 2020 presidential election and the false allegations of electoral fraud he spread. He instigated the "Assault on the Capitol" on January 6, 2021, in which his supporters tried to prevent election certification. Trump's attacks on the independence of the judiciary, as well as his attempts to influence investigations against his government or himself, has also shaken confidence in the rule of law.

During his presidency there were numerous accusations of corruption and conflicts of interest, for example in connection with his business and the influence that his family and group had on his political decisions. Trump is known for his lack of transparency and for withholding information, especially on important issues such as the response to the pandemic or in connection with secret information. His close relations with autocratic leaders such as Vladimir Putin, Kim Jong-un and others underscore how he is courting authoritarian regimes while ignoring the values of democracy and human rights, raising doubts about his stance on international standards and norms.

The drastically changed geopolitical situation creates a kind of pincer feeling for Europe, caught between the superpowers Russia and the USA, but also exposed to the activities of China. Only a common foreign and security policy and a coordinated approach to economic relations, defence and trade strategy can ensure Europe's ability to act freely.

The Russian leadership, that exalted circle of people who

thrive on a quasi-godlike understanding of geopolitical maneuvering, looks at the Western, chaotic White House in Washington with an admirable mixture of capriciousness and composure. And who could enjoy the taste in a moment like this better than the Kremlin, when he observes the colorful spectacle of Trump's escapades. Vladimir Putin is reclining in his leather chair, an invisible grin on his face as he gazes at the latest Twitter news from Donald Trump that once again shakes the political worldview of a democratic country. One could almost get the impression that the Russian president, instead of shifting the worries of a war, at this moment is more enjoying the ripe apple when he tastes the stupidities from the US world.

Putin may taste Trump's international politics as a unique dilettantism that drives the entire Western political establishment to madness in its own way. The Russian leadership is not only laughing at the unpredictable Twitter outbursts and Trump's opaque manoeuvres, it is also using them as a kind of amusing, if disturbing, distraction from its own geopolitical goals.

Trump, this bizarre game ball of American politics, is seen in the circles of the Kremlin as a reluctant clown. No doubt, the ironic joy of his solo is interpreted as a kind of happy mess that allows the Kremlin to pursue its own plan in the background. Here is a man who is the world's most agitated and the Russian strategists enjoy the idea that the American political system is run by a chaotic one.

Trump should, according to the dream of the Kremlin acrobats, really go golfing more often and leave the rest to them. The scent of the coons hangs in the air, while one is guided by an adventurous dilettante. The Russian leadership could hardly do better. While the West is embroiled in its own conflicts, the Kremlin's superiors can quietly and relish the next act of this political drama. Trump's America-First policy in Moscow may even be reformulated as "Russia first". Perhaps one day he will receive a Russian award for his efforts to achieve national sovereignty.

What a delicious spectacle! In a world where political hostilities are usually fought with the sharpness of a dagger, Trump seems to have almost become an involuntary ally in the eyes of the Kremlin. The man at the head of the White House may have mysteriously become a puppet in a global play where the true director behind the scenes, in Russian tradition, controls the big political chessboard. The Trump Award for National Sovereignty would probably be a highly acclaimed event in Moscow, perhaps a gold medal given to Trump symbolically for his remarkable ability to isolate America from international dialogue and at the same time to increase Russian influence on the world stage.

But beware, the spectacle could take an unexpected turn, if this American narcissist suddenly smells of a fuse. It is a dangerous game, in which you can never be sure when the wild tiger will awaken in him. Once Trump perceives the smell of threat in the air, it may well be that something will happen, which Trump accused Ukrainian president Selensky of: "You are playing with World War III". It could suddenly feel like a dark omen. Those who have followed American policy know that Trump is always in a position to step on the stage and inflame or at least exacerbate an international conflict with one of his famous, provocative tweets.

Where Putin may be acting with cool, though satanic calculation, Trump might rather decide in an emotional, spontaneous moment to press the red button to at least verbally destabilize his opponents. And this is not an easy game. Those who make the wrong moves on this geopolitical chessboard could trigger the wildest fears ever thought possible. Of course, Moscow will still rub its fingers as long as Trump remains an unpredictable factor in the West.

But at the same time, the Russian leaders may look with

a certain thrill at the possibility that this cowboy might one day in his own dangerous way ignite the war he so often accused others of. The sweet scent of malice could quickly turn into the sour taste of fear, should the self-proclaimed anti-establishment rebel really feel pushed into the corner and dare the ultimate act of a geopolitical escalation.

The nation's madcap, who may be holding on so strongly to his power because he is constantly surrounded by threats or dangers, could of course make a u-turn, precisely when it suits him least. He could at any time turn the swivel chair 180 degrees and suddenly appear as the greatest reformer. The world could be amazed at how, in a moment of realization, the iron grip on power turns into a generous change of course that suddenly upholds democracy and freedom of expression. Perhaps the coward is suddenly overcome by a visionary moment and realizes that the self-determination of people are the true key to a successful future, of course while he is on the safe side in a thoroughly controlled system.

A leader who is known for his authoritarian traits could suddenly change his attitude out of nothing, as if he had recognized the danger for himself, perhaps because the pressure from outside has become so great that he can no longer help, to take the democratic path. But let's not be fooled, the sudden turnaround could just as quickly reverse itself when the threat has passed.

And what does Europe do when the Italian Prime Minister, Giorgia Meloni, who has so far been a good advocate of reason in the European Union, shows her true face and sticks to fascist cooperations? She has never made a secret of her positive attitude towards Donald Trump. She has repeatedly admired him as a figure fighting for national sovereignty and against the globalist agenda. In him she saw a strong, unconventional leader who has taken the Western world out of its political comfort zone. Their sympathy for Trump is not surprising in many ways, as they themselves operate in a similar political direction and have many of their political goals and rhetoric parallel to those of Trump.

Meloni's relationship with Trump and her political allies may seem to many as a deliberately calculated strategy that will help her gain a wider following, especially in a Europe which is struggling with growing nationalism and populist movements. Her admiration for Trump could serve as a kind of political legitimation that opens some doors in a world of international diplomacy, especially if she wants to distance herself from the EU or the established political class.

However, this attitude could become increasingly problematic in the EU and other Western countries if it moves further towards more radical, authoritarian thinking. At a time when right-wing populism is gaining traction in Europe, Melanie's closeness to Trump could help her position herself as part of an international network of anti-establishment leaders. But this is where the danger arises.

It's a complex balance that Meloni is trying to master. On the one hand, she shows sympathy for populist, nationalist movements; on the other hand, she must assert herself as a serious political leader in the EU. If their sympathies for Trump and more radical forces within the EU continue to grow, they could be put under pressure, especially when the EU stresses that their course may pose a threat to democracy and European values.

Be that as it may, Meloni's positive attitude towards Trump will always remain a double-edged sword, a weapon that could help her in the international game but also carries a risk if she pushes too much in this direction. Time will tell whether it preserves political reason or is finally infected by the darker currents of political radicalism.

It would be a dramatic plot twist in the European political landscape! Giorgia Meloni, hitherto perceived by many as a supposedly sensible leader of the Italian

government, who has appeared in the European Union
with a certain moderation and pragmatism, could
suddenly take a dark turn and show her true face. The
idea that it is based on fascist cooperation or at least
seeks an approach to such forces is a disturbing thought
for many who have believed in their previous positions
and rhetoric.

One could imagine how the political scene in Europe
would react to this. The entire balance that has been on
a fine line between progressivity and conservative forces
in the Union for years could be shaken. European
cooperation would certainly be under pressure, and
Meloni would have a strong ally at her side with Marie-
Le Pen/Bardella. It would be an extremely important and
potentially explosive alliance in European politics. Both
have similar political agendas, from national sovereignty
to a restrictive immigration policy and the rejection of
the so-called globalist project. Their cooperation could
thus trigger a huge political current within the EU,
especially at a time when nationalism is gaining ground

in some European countries.

Meloni and Le Pen could develop into a kind of axis of the right-wing movement that gains influence not only in their home countries, but also throughout the EU. Their political chemistry would be based in many ways on the common rejection of the EU bureaucracy and the established political elites. Both women represent, albeit in slightly different ways, a view that questions the European integration process and prioritizes national interests.

A stronger merger between Meloni and Bardella, Le Pen's comrade-in-arms and supposed successor could significantly change the political landscape of the EU. Their voices would have more weight in the institutions of the Union, from the European Parliament to the intergovernmental conferences. It could become a serious test for the coherence and stability of the EU, as the two women are often at odds with the pro-European majority in their political agendas. You could try to steer the EU's political direction in a direction less of Brussels and more of national sovereignty.

And they quickly had the footboard rider Orbán from Hungary at their side, a rather dangerous constellation: Meloni, Le Pen/Bardella and Viktor Orbán. The Hungarian prime minister, who has been a prominent representative of the right-wing populist and nationalist wing in Europe for years, has repeatedly shown himself to be an annoying troublemaker on the European scene in recent years. On the one hand, he has established himself as the father of the nation by acting as a strong advocate of the "illiberal state" against European politics and Western liberalism. On the other hand, he has often used the opportunity to ingratiate himself with the EU and other Western partners. Orbán has repeatedly stressed that he is a European but also a Hungarian nationalist, ready to fight against the rules and values imposed by Brussels.

A connivance of Meloni and Le Pen would strengthen

Orbán in his political position and possibly give him a greater platform to further expand his policy of national sovereignty and resistance against the liberal Western order. Together, they could form an even louder, more articulated front against the EU's liberal mainstream, with a common agenda that may push for the end of United Europe.

However, it should also be noted that both politicians, although they have many political intersections, are not always completely in agreement on all issues. Their national policies and how they deal with certain issues, such as economic policy or social issues, could be different in nature, which might also make cooperation between them more difficult. But even a looser cooperation or an ideological exchange would be enough to change the political dynamics in Europe and to really upset the current order.

The reactions would be as rapid as they were dramatic. The EU, which has often had to ask how far it can go with member states when it comes to democratic principles and the protection of human rights, would probably not hesitate long to voice its concerns loudly. A drift of Melonis into extreme cooperations could lead to a massive loss of confidence in their policies. But here comes the interesting, almost fascinating aspect: how much could Meloni actually depend on the power of the EU? Should they start to move purposefully in a direction that is perceived as fascist or authoritarian, this could not only lead to a dramatic political spread within Italy, but also challenge the EU's role in upholding democratic standards. Italy, as one of the most important and influential nations in Europe, could sweep the Union like a storm through such cooperation.

That would be a real test for the European institutions to see if they could deal with a country like Italy in this new, more dangerous direction without endangering the Union itself. And not to forget, Meloni's pragmatic policy approach could suddenly turn out to be a political move in which she not only wants to assert herself as a serious actor in the EU, but also seeks reassurance on the side of radical forces, to consolidate their power inside and outside the country. And yet the question remains whether she would really be willing to play this game. The political arena is full of tactical maneuvers and how it moves in this delicate situation will be decisive for its future and that of Italian democracy. She could walk on this thin line between the sensible politician and a more dangerous, radical version of herself. And as she plays with it, Europe may hold its breath in growing concern.

At this point it should be emphasized again, in the historical context, one can see how difficult it is to keep a clear view of tacticians and psychotic followers in a mixture of impenetrable tacticians. It would be beneficial to clearly recognize the moves in the game, as they can signal the approaching storm clouds of societal developments. Early detection would be advantageous in order to avoid being too late to react.

It is a great challenge to navigate in an environment

characterized by opaque actors and unpredictable dynamics. Historically, there are always periods when it is difficult to recognize the true motives and intentions of individuals and groups that may be driven by self-interest or psychological confusion.

The ability to recognize the movements of those who act in such complex social and political situations is crucial for understanding the possible consequences and dangers at an early stage. Often there are inconspicuous hints and subliminal signals that warn of major social upheavals. A keen understanding of these dynamics can not only serve as a shield against late reaction, but also help to take proactive measures before the dark clouds of a social storm become too large.

Combining the feeling of professional experience with the well-founded, evidence-based knowledge from evaluations, would create a particularly strong basis for informed decisions and assessments. In many complex, fast-developing scenarios it is crucial to resort to both intuition and experiential knowledge, often honed by years of practice and the hard data and analysis results, that come from systematic evaluations.

It would be time to apply evidence-based practices in the spheres of elected mandate holders, that is, to work with an approach that bases decisions on scientifically sound, evaluated data. Combining these two levels creates a stronger basis for preventive action and, if necessary, early reaction to developments. The backwardness of party-bound practice is pointed out in the book „Parties - sources of nonsense" *)

In many areas, be it environmental policy, health care, education or social justice, especially in international relations, decisions could be based on scientifically validated knowledge and thus be made much more efficient and future-oriented. The advantage of this

*) Parties - sources of nonsense
  Europe's way into the future ISBN 9783769355505

approach is that it puts not only political interests, but also and above all the actual needs and developments within society in the foreground.

Europe has recognized, late but definitely, that it needs to strengthen its defense capabilities and resilience. Europe should strive for greater independence from unilateral energy sources. This could be done by investing in renewable energy, diversifying energy sources and working more closely together on the energy transition. Europe can also expand its influence through completely new alliances with different countries and regions worldwide and make itself independent of individual great powers.

A common European response is needed, not only through holey sanctions but also through clear military presence on the borders and in unstable regions such as Ukraine or the Baltic Sea. Should Russia threaten the international order, Europe could take immediate action, such as military support for threatened states. Europe should be tougher and more confident in its economic policies, especially with regard to China and Russia. Economic sanctions and trade wars are important tools to reduce the influence of authoritarian regimes.

If US foreign policy under certain governments reverts back to nationalist or isolated positions, Europe could move to impose critical economic sanctions against the US in order to protect its own interests. Europe must not see itself as an extension of US foreign policy. Above all, Europe should stop seeing itself as a buffer zone between the great powers. Instead, Europe must be active on the world stage and position itself as one of the leading global powers. Europe could enter into strategic alliances with regional players like India, Japan, Canada, Australia, which have similar geopolitical interests. A strong counterweight to China, Russia and the US can only be achieved by building a global bloc of democratic and strategic partners. Civil societies and democratic institutions must be protected by a strong political will.

And Xi Jinping in China? Under him, political power within the Chinese Communist Party has increasingly focused on himself. He has established himself as the core of the party and has increasingly stepped out of the collegiality of the leadership in recent years. This trend was further reinforced by the abolition of the term limit for the 2018 Presidium, which means that he can theoretically remain in office indefinitely.

Xi has consolidated all major political institutions under his control, from the government to the army and the party. The power of state leadership was further strengthened by the formation of control bodies to combat corruption within the party, but also as a means to eliminate political opponents and secure the power base. Under Xi Jinping, censorship in China was massively expanded. The government strictly monitors and controls the internet and social media to suppress critical voices and prevent dissent. There are extensive censorship measures that are also applied to literature, art and research. The Great Firewall is constantly being expanded to control access to information from abroad. A striking feature of his regime is the harsh repression of ethnic and religious minorities, such as the Uighurs in Xinjiang, the Tibetans or the Falun Gong movement. In Xinjiang, Uyghurs and other Muslim minorities are held in re-education camps and repressed through surveillance, forced labour and cultural assimilation.

Another element of Xi Jinping's policy is the expansion of surveillance states. The use of technology to monitor the population and support autocratic regimes worldwide shows how China exports its political principles. There is much discussion about how Chinese companies like Huawei or ZTE cooperate with the Chinese government and are seen as strategic tools of influence. The increasing integration of these companies into other countries' critical infrastructures will pose long-term security risks.

Tiandy Technologies, a prominent Chinese video surveillance company, has come under international scrutiny due to its alleged involvement in human rights abuses against Uyghur muslims and other minority groups in China's Xinjiang region. Reports indicate that Tiandy's products, including facial recognition software capable of detecting ethnicity, have been utilized by Chinese authorities to monitor and suppress Uyghur populations.Tiandy's growing international footprint exemplifies China's broader strategy of exporting surveillance technologies to foreign government, often in developing countries or autocratic regime, under the umbrella of smart city and public security initiatives. These exports strengthen China's political influence abroad, contribute to the normalization of authoritarian technology policies and risk enabling human rights violations around the world.

Xi Jinping is pursuing an increasingly aggressive foreign policy, which aims to establish China as a dominant world power. It also shows its authoritarian character, for example in dealing with Taiwan, Hong Kong or the South China Sea. Militarisation and the emphasis on national security and sovereignty reflect authoritarian attitudes.

Despite his charismatic appearance and his famously deceptively friendly smile, China's undisputed leader pursues an economic colonial policy with which he economically subjugates governments, especially in the Global South. And China's so-called New Silk Road or the Belt and Road Initiative is a striking example of this economic colonialism. On velvety, or rather on silken paws, the Chinese dragon creeps into the countries of the global south.The aim of this initiative is to expand China's influence in strategic regions by making massive investments in infrastructure projects in many developing countries, often coupled with huge loans. These loans drive the countries concerned into a debt trap that allows China to exercise political and economic control when the debtor states have difficulties to settle their debts.

China pursues an aggressive foreign economic policy,

often referred to as neo-colonial. The massive use of credit in developing countries, combined with strategic investments, gives China not only access to important raw materials but also political influence. If these countries fall into a debt trap, China will be able to influence political decisions in these countries through economic means, whether through land transfers, commodity contracts or access to military and strategic positions. This is a very clever, but also very risky strategy aimed at shifting the global balance of power.

Another problem is the sustainability of these projects. Many of the construction projects financed by China, such as bridges or roads, are often not adapted to local needs and may be economically unsustainable in the long term. The criticized „white-elephant-projects", which cost a lot of money but bring little benefit, are an example of this type of development. The crucial question remains whether this type of economic support for developing countries actually leads to sustainable development or whether it leads to a dependence on

China that harms the affected countries in the long term.

In some cases, such as Sri Lanka, this has already led to situations where countries have had to cede land and strategic resources to China in order to settle their debts. Critics describe this practice as debt-trap diplomacy and accuse China of pursuing in a modern context power strategies similar to those used during the colonial era, but in economic form. Instead of military expansion, what is now being sought is a form of economic domination in which the countries concerned become dependent on China's influence in the long term.

So what could be done to counteract these potential negative effects? A first step could be to increase transparency and fairness in international negotiations. It might also be useful for these countries to invest in more sustainable, long-term viable solutions together with international partners such as the World Bank or the African Development Bank so that they do not become dependent on a single power.

China pursues a policy that challenges international norms and institutions. In matters such as human rights, censorship or territorial claims for example in the South China Sea, China often acts contrary to global ideals. Xi Jinping shows little interest in international agreements that could limit China's influence and is willing to respond to pressure, which puts the Western world in a difficult position. This attitude presents a challenge for countries, who are interested in international cooperation and the rules of global trade.

China uses its economic power not only to invest directly in countries, but also to influence them politically. States that are economically dependent on China may be under pressure in international forums, such as the United Nations or the World Health Organization, to advocate political positions that favor Chinese interests. There are reports that China uses economic incentives to induce countries to make certain diplomatic decisions or, conversely, to cut off diplomatic relations if a country does not behave in accordance with China's political ideas.

The cautious attitude towards China's policies is therefore necessary because this policy pursues a strategic plan that goes far beyond short-term economic benefits. It is not just an economic expansion, but a comprehensive geopolitical agenda, that aims to change the international order in favor of China. The challenge for the international community is how to cooperate with China in areas such as trade and climate change, while ensuring that that the international norms and sovereignty of the countries concerned are not undermined by China's economic power.

A cautious and critical stance toward China's policies is not merely justified, it is an obligation rooted in strategic foresight and democratic responsibility. Those who view China's global engagement purely through the lens of economics fail to grasp the deeper geopolitical ambitions that underpin the actions of its leadership. This is not just about trade, investment or technological cooperation. It is about influence, control and the long-term projection of power with the clear objective of reshaping global norms in favor of authoritarian governance.

China's policies follow a calculated and long-term strategy executed with discipline and persistence. Economic partnerships, such as those promoted through the Belt and Road Initiative, are not just infrastructure investments. They are tools for cultivating political dependencies. When China finances ports, power grids or telecommunication infrastructure in Europe, Africa, or Asia, it is not doing so out of goodwill. It is securing leverage, influence, and, when necessary, the means to coerce.

Simultaneously, China is advancing its technological dominance with massive state subsidies, protectionist policies and frequent violations of fair competition rules.

Strategic sectors, such as artificial intelligence, quantum computing, and semiconductors, have become battlegrounds in a systemic conflict between democratic resilience and authoritarian ambition. Anyone who assumes mutual benefit without addressing this imbalance risks surrendering not only technological sovereignty but also long-term political independence.

Perhaps most concerning is the way China strategically blurs the line between economics and politics, a textbook case of geo-economic power projection. Trade becomes a weapon. Political criticism is met with economic retaliation. Just look at the punitive measures taken against countries like Lithuania or Australia following their independent political decisions that displeased Beijing. This is not diplomacy. It is coercion under the guise of cooperation.

So it is not only a question of how to deal with China's economic expansion, but also how to preserve the political and ideological sovereignty of one's own societies and the global community. If the international community remains too passive or reacts too late to geopolitical developments, China willc further expand its economic and political dominance and change the rules of the game in its own favor.

Europe must not fall into the trap of comfortable dependence. The term "risk reduction" must not degenerate into a diplomatic smokescreen. It must be backed up by concrete actions. Diversifying trade relations, investing in strategic autonomy in key industries and establishing clear boundaries against authoritarian interventions are essential. Business relationships can only be successful if they are based on reciprocity, transparency and shared values, not on dependence and opportunism. After all, those who remain silent today for short-term economic reasons risk giving up their political autonomy tomorrow.

The greatest danger lies not in the power of these regimes, but in the hesitation of democracies and their economies to respond. Too often, fear of escalation or loss of economic opportunity leads to silence, appeasement, or complicity. This is the cowardice of comfort, a reluctance to confront hard truths when they threaten short-term interests. But history teaches that accommodating dictatorships only emboldens them. When democracies fail to draw clear lines, they invite further aggression.

Companies operating globally need to closely monitor geopolitical risks and include them in their strategic calculations. This includes not only economic risks, but also political, social and legal risks. With regard to China, for example, companies that are involved in projects under the Belt and Road Initiative or have business relationships with Chinese companies, forced to question the political orientation and ethical implications of their partnerships. Human rights, environmental standards and transparency are issues that should be considered when evaluating partnerships and investments.

If companies ignore these geopolitical factors, they risk not only legal consequences but also a erosion of trust in their brand. Effective compliance management is essential to ensure that companies comply with legal, ethical and regulatory requirements in all countries where they operate. Especially in an increasingly networked world where international standards and multinational regulations are becoming more relevant, companies must consider not only local but also global compliance requirements. The trust of consumers and investors is strongly linked to a company's value-oriented decisions.

The geopolitical and economic challenges facing China and other globally influential nations require a complex and cautious approach by companies. Only through a strategic integration of compliance, a clear corporate identity that reflects ethical principles and open communication about risks and assessments can companies ensure that they are not only successful in a volatile global market, but also take responsibility and build long-term sustainable relationships.

In addition to consumers, investors are increasingly looking for companies that are not only profitable but also operate ethically and sustainably. The trend towards environmental, social and governance ESG-investments is another example of civil society's growing influence on the business sector. Investors increasingly want to invest in companies that take their social responsibility seriously and consider the impact of their business practices on society and the environment. ESG criteria have now become so important that they not only influence the financial market, but can also determine a company's market access.

12. CONFRONTATION WITH DICTATORSHIPS

Confrontation does not mean war. It means clarity, conviction and coordinated action. It means defending truth in the face of disinformation, protecting vulnerable states from authoritarian pressure, reducing strategic dependencies, whether on energy, technology, or capital and perhaps most importantly, strengthening the democratic model from within. Because a democracy that cannot defend itself morally and institutionally will always be vulnerable to external threats.

Hope, in this context, is not a passive belief in a better future, it is an active defiance of inevitability. To confront dictatorship is to affirm that freedom, dignity and justice are not outdated ideals, but the foundation of lasting peace and human flourishing. Silence is no longer neutral. In the confrontation between dictatorship and democracy, inaction is a form of surrender.

How can we defend ourselves against devastating developments in international affairs? To arm themselves against economic blackmail and the impact of geopolitical tensions, countries should diversify their economies across sectors and trading partners. A broader range of partners and products makes countries more resilient to the effects of trade wars, sanctions or unilateral political decisions.

Several units should build strategic alliances with others that share similar values, such as democracy, human rights and the rule of law. In this way, they can work together to impose economic sanctions that are internationally oriented or to create alternative economic structures that are less dependent on authoritarian powers.

A strong civil society that does not give up is one of the most effective protective mechanisms against authoritarian tendencies. Protecting freedom of expression, supporting independent media, encouraging popular engagement and building network structures for democracy can help keep authoritarian governments in check and mobilize public resistance. In an environment of rapid disinformation and manipulation, societies should place great emphasis on education and media literacy to enable their citizens to recognize misinformation and understand the political consequences of authoritarian actions. Well-informed citizens are a bulwark against populist and authoritarian movements.

International understanding and intercultural dialog are crucial to reduce tensions and avoid misunderstandings. Programs that promote intercultural exchange can help reduce prejudice and hostility and create a stronger global network of like-minded countries and societies. In addition, countries can defend themselves against the increasing influence of authoritarian states in the field of technology by investing in their own digital infrastructure. This includes developing their own alternatives to global technologies controlled by authoritarian regimes.

Swarm intelligence, originally a concept from biology that deals with the collective behavior of animals in large groups, is increasingly being applied to human societies. In international politics, especially in relation to dictatorships, swarm intelligence can promote the formation of alliances and networks between states and international organizations. By sharing information and resources, countries taking action against dictatorial regimes can work together effectively. Sharing intelligence on human rights abuses or corruption can lead to international pressure on such regimes and isolate them.

Swarm intelligence can also act as a mechanism of economic and political pressure on dictatorships. If a global consensus emerges on how to deal with an autocratic regime, for example through sanctions, diplomatic isolation or support for opposition members, this collective approach can be an effective means of forcing change. In general, swarm intelligence refers to the collective behaviour of decentrally organized systems in which individual actors react to simple rules, resulting in a complex, intelligent overall system. In international politics and international relations, the concept of swarm intelligence is a metaphor for the way in which states, international organizations and actors respond collectively to global threats. Collaboration, information sharing and resource pooling are critical to developing a rapid and effective response to the crisis.

Swarm intelligence is becoming important in peacekeeping. This involves various actors, from states to NGOs and international organizations, working together on solutions to construct stable peace processes. International relations are increasingly permeated by network-like structures in which states are linked not only bilaterally but also multilaterally. What is needed today are strong alliances that prioritize efficiency, not fragmented bilateral arrangements. The driving force behind cooperation must be the shared rational interests of security and collective wellbeing, whether at the level of macro-regions, nation-states, or provinces. In contrast, separatism and the fragmentation into small mosaic-like entities only serve to reinforce harmful nationalist ideologies, which can have serious and far-reaching consequences. Unity through pragmatic collaboration is the sustainable path forward in an increasingly interconnected world.In such a network, everyone can contribute to the overall solution of a problem through their actions and interactions. Such networks promote swarm intelligence because they are based on the idea that the collective intelligence of many participants is stronger than that of individual actors.

The idea of global commitment involves states and international institutions working together to tackle cross-border problems such as climate change, refugee crises or the fight against terrorism. The success of this type of cooperation is often based on the principles of swarm intelligence, in which many actors pool their resources, expertise and perspectives in order to find solutions. Cooperation and interdependence form a dynamic system that exhibits similar principles to swarm intelligence. Individual states are often not able to solve global problems in isolation, but must work together in a cooperative network.

13. EFFICIENCY AND INEFFICIENCY
OF EUROPEAN INSTITUTIONS

This requires a tour d'horizon into European history. *)
The observation that political structures were effective,
even peaceful and above all powerful and prosperous
when they were massive and widespread is unequivocal.
This was true for the beginning of the important
civilizations of antiquity as well as in the later epochs of
the Middle Ages or the modern period.

This observation is an important key to understanding
the effectiveness of political structures, especially their
ability to consolidate peace and prosperity. The
prosperous Europe has always been linked to its size and
reach. From the first civilizations of antiquity to
developments in the Middle Ages and the modern era,
the expansion of political systems played a decisive role.

*) The Psyche of World History ISBN 9783757810108

The same principle applied in the Ottoman Empire, in the Chinese dynasties, in South America or wherever.

Already in ancient times, great empires such as the Roman Empire or the Persian Empire, which were based on massive geographical expansions, saw their serenity and prosperity in common strength. Their political structures were designed to manage vast areas, integrate different peoples and cultures and distribute resources effectively. The Roman Empire was able to build an extensive administration that was central to the peace and prosperity that historians call "Pax Romana". This structure made it possible to secure a stable, long-lasting peace in a vast area through efficient infrastructure, jurisdiction and military presence.

In the Middle Ages, the Holy Roman Empire was such a construct that, although it is considered by many to be inefficient because of its federal structure, it nevertheless lasted for centuries. The feudal system, which prevailed in large parts of medieval Europe, provided a wide distribution of power and responsibility, with local rulers directly connected to monarchs or emperors.

The birth of a united Europe was the kingdom of Charlemagne, when there was no division into Germans and French. Only the struggles for succession, the splitting of the empire into countless duchies and counties contributed to massive division battles. Narrow national thinking began only in 1871 with the founding of the German Empire and found its destructive culmination in the Nazi regime of Germany and in the Second World War.

In modern times there was a greater centralization of power, for example in the French absolutism under Louis XIV or in the British Empire. These states began to develop institutions and administrative systems that promised efficient administration and control of an expanding empire. But they failed because of their own desires for power and their plans to conquer colonies.

Their debacle began with an inability to think positively in large spaces, and they ended up sinking into the morass of power.

The experience of the Second World War and the destruction it caused, after 1945, finally led to a new vision of a united Europe based on cooperation and peace, A vision expressed in the founding of the European Union and other international organisations. The transition from a Europe that under Charlemagne saw itself as a cultural and political centre, to a Europe of nation states, which in 19th and 20th century was marked by conflict, shows how the political landscape has changed over the centuries. Today, this story is a reminder of the importance of working together at European level to avoid repeating past mistakes.
In the modern era, the European Union could be seen as a new form of a far-reaching political entity based on the principle of economic and political integration. The EU today is an example of the idea of creating a large political structure that relies on cooperation and co-

creation to promote peace and prosperity. In many ways, the EU is an attempt to avoid the mistakes of the past such as the fragmentation of Europe in history or the destructive wars of modern times, by reconciling a comprehensive political structure with a variety of specific interests.

The historical review of the creation of modern Europe is indeed fascinating when one considers the visions and political vision of the great thinkers and statesmen of that time. After the destruction of World War II, it was crucial to rebuilt Europe not only economically but also politically. In this crucial phase, a number of politicians and visionaries emerged who laid the foundation for today's Europe. Richard von Coudenhove-Kalergi represented the visionary, the philosopher of unity. As the founder of the Pan-European Movement already in the 1920s, Coudenhove-Kalergi imagined a supranational political order that could transcend nationalism and war, uniting Europe's nations under a shared cultural and political framework. Jean Monnet's vision is more relevant than ever. As one of the founding architects of European integration, Monnet understood that cooperation among nations could not rely on lofty declarations or idealism alone, it required institutions, procedures and above all, structured political management.

Alcide de Gasperi, the Italian Prime Minister after the war, advocated for close cooperation between European states and was a supporter of the establishment of the European Coal and Steel Community, which is considered the first step toward the economic integration of Europe. Jean Monnet and Robert Schuman, also key figures in the early European integration, recognized the need for a common European economic policy to secure peace and create a stable economic foundation. The Schuman Declaration of 1950 led to the creation of the ECSC, which later became the foundation for the European Economic Community and the present European Union.

The former french President Charles de Gaulle dreamed once of a "Europe from the Atlantic to the Urals," reflecting his vision of a united continent capable of acting independently of the superpowers of the USA and the Soviet Union. He indeed had a vision of a united Europe, but he referred to it as a "Europe of the peoples," which mistakenly positioned him as an opponent of European integration. Otto von Habsburg was a passionate advocate for European unity and campaigned for the reunification of continental Europe, viewing the idea of a United Europe as a solution to many of the political and ethnic conflicts that had plagued Europe in the past. Helmut Kohl, the German Chancellor, was one of the architects of the reunification of Germany and played a key role in the political process of European integration, particularly through his support for European unity and the Maastricht Treaty of 1992, which created the European Union.

These politicians and visionaries, through their ideas and political initiatives, helped lay the foundations for modern Europe. Their cooperation, despite differing national interests, provided the fundamental ideas for a peace order and created the concept of a political framework in which cooperation and solidarity are central. The political vision of a united Europe enabled the overcoming of past conflicts and the creation of a new, peaceful era.

The concept of efficiency and inefficiency in European institutions is closely tied to this historical development and the structural changes in political organizations in Europe. In the past, it has been shown that political structures were particularly successful and stable when they had a wide-reaching, comprehensive network of institutions and administrative structures. This led to greater cohesion and better resource distribution, which was of great importance during times of peace and prosperity.

The administrative apparatus of the EU, which is often perceived as bureaucratic, is frequently regarded as inefficient, especially when it comes to making quick decisions or implementing political measures. On the other hand, due to its extensive institutions and the ability to act at various levels - local, national, and European - the EU is also capable of integrating a wide range of interests, thereby achieving broad consensus.

The perceived inefficiency of the EU is often attributed to the political inefficiency of the nation-states. In the early phases of European integration, when the EU was still in its infancy, many political positions were taken by former, retired politicians. These politicians were often less able to develop the political influence, vision, and determination required for shaping and implementing effective European policies.

The challenge for the EU lies not only in the institutional structures but also in the complexity of the political landscape, where national interests often conflict with overarching European goals, leading to political paralysis. The political will for European integration must be regularly confirmed and supported by the member states. In this sense, it becomes clear that the true inefficiency of the EU is often less caused by the institutional structures themselves, but by the political reality in which national sovereignty and European interests need to be balanced.

However, a shift in perspective has since occurred and many of the politicians representing the EU today are politically more influential and better connected, both at the national and European levels. Particularly, the new internationally well-educated generation gives legitimate hope for substantial progress in the management of European institutions. Things are changing, EU politics isn't just about bureaucracy anymore. A new wave of better-connected, better-educated politicians is stepping up, and many of them have real clout both at home and in Brussels. This new generation, shaped by international education and experience, could finally bring the kind of fresh leadership the EU's been needing for a long time.

Many of today's political actors in the EU are not only more experienced and politically influential but also better connected at the European levels. This networking is a crucial advantage, as it facilitates the exchange of ideas and collaboration across borders, which is essential for a multi-layered political union like the EU. Particularly noticeable is the increasing presence of a new generation of politicians who are internationally educated and well-connected in the globalized world. Many of these actors not only have a deep understanding of the complex challenges Europe faces but also the ability to think beyond national interests and develop solutions at the European level. These politicians have a strong international perspective and are able to represent the EU better in European and global contexts.

The new generation, often more familiar with digital technologies, global trends and intercultural communication, brings fresh ideas and perspectives into the EU's political decision-making processes. Their international education and experience in various political and economic systems help in developing new approaches that are significant at the European and global levels. These young, dynamic leaders could help position the EU better in an increasingly multipolar world, making it a more coherent and flexible political entity.

With the involvement of these politically well-educated and connected actors, there is growing hope that the EU may be able to meet the challenges it faces today with greater flexibility and efficiency. In particular, the new generations are capable of developing quick, innovative solutions to current and future problems, whether in the areas of economics, climate change, digital transformation or geopolitical uncertainty.

Such progress could be realized at various levels, whether through the modernization of EU institutions, a stronger emphasis on inter-institutional cooperation, or a more coordinated European foreign policy. An more effective decision-making process within the EU, which takes into account the various interests of the individual units and, with the help of modern evaluation mechanisms, enables a quicker response to crises, is also increasingly seen as an area where progress must be made.

There is a growing recognition that the EU needs institutional and structural reforms to make decision-making more efficient. Measures such as simplifying voting processes, optimizing cooperation between EU institutions and member regions, and improving transparency and communication between political actors are crucial. Faster action could also be enabled by increasing the use of majority decisions in certain areas, rather than relying on unanimous decisions that often lead to blockages.

The efficiency of the European Union could be optimized through the establishment of early warning systems and the use of innovative data analysis technologies, enabling the EU to detect potential crises early and respond accordingly. Enhanced cooperation with external experts could also help develop well-informed, quickly implementable solutions. Furthermore, so-called crisis mechanisms within EU institutions could be established, specifically designed for swift handling of emergencies. These provisions could allow European institutions to react flexibly to crises without having to engage the entire institutional structure extensively. Such a program would also improve coordination between the individual units and the EU institutions, thereby increasing the efficiency of the response.

The greatest challenge in implementing more effective decision-making and crisis management within the EU lies in maintaining the balance between efficiency and the principles of democratic participation. Therefore, the EU must continue to ensure that all groups and regions are involved in the decision-making process, without losing its ability to respond quickly in critical situations. If the EU succeeds in reforming its structures to make decisions that are both quick and consensus-oriented, it will not only improve its responsiveness in times of crisis but also its ability to act as a united entity in an increasingly complex and dynamic world.

14. WHAT DO EUROPEAN POLITICIANS FEAR MOST?

European politicians fear a variety of challenges that stem from internal and external sources. These fears reflect the complex political, economic, and social landscape in which the EU operates. A central issue that concerns many European politicians is the rise of populism and nationalism. Populist and nationalist movements challenge the EU and its values, advocating a return to national power politics. Many politicians fear that these movements could weaken European integration and lead to the fragmentation of the Union. Brexit, in particular, demonstrated how dangerous national movements can be for European unity.

Another important issue is the question of European identity. Politicians fear that these tensions could lead to a growing alienation between citizens and the European institutions. The collapse of the European dream could threaten political cohesion and confidence in the EUuropen Union. The question of European identity becomes particularly relevant in times of political and economic uncertainty. While the European Union continues to grow closer on an institutional level, many citizens still lack a strong sense of belonging to a shared European project. National identities remain dominant in the political and social consciousness, often overshadowing European values and a collective sense of unity. To ensure long-term stability and cohesion, the EU needs more than just institutional reforms, it must actively promote a European public sphere. This could be achieved through targeted initiatives in education, cross-border media projects, and increased cultural exchange.

To meet these challenges, it is crucial that the institutions act transparently and give citizens the opportunity to actively participate in decision-making processes. The focus should be on the common European value system. The collapse of the European vision could not only threaten political stability, but also have economic and social consequences that go far beyond the EU's borders. It is therefore important that the European institutions take proactive measures to strengthen citizens' trust and promote a positive European identity.European politicians also fear that the EU could lose influence in the increasingly multipolar world order if it does not strengthen its foreign policy coherence. The inability to agree on a unified foreign policy could weaken the Union's reputation and capacity for action on the global stage.

The rapid development of technologies, especially artificial intelligence and digitalisation, is one of the biggest challenges for European policymakers. On the one hand, these technologies offer a huge potential for innovation and growth, but on the other hand they bring about profound social and economic changes that are not always easy to manage. The fear is that Europe could fall behind other global powers such as the US and China in the digital and technological field if it fails to create the right policy framework.

Sovereignty is indeed one of the most charged and romanticized concepts in the world of international politics. At its core, sovereignty represents a nation's ability to govern itself, make decisions independently, and retain control over its territory, resources and policies without external interference. For many, this idealized vision of sovereignty evokes a sense of national pride and autonomy, a belief that the true essence of a nation lies in its ability to determine its own fate without foreign influence. However, this romanticized notion of sovereignty contrasts sharply with the realities of an increasingly interconnected and globalized world.

Sovereignty, the romanticized ideal of complete independence, which in reality often seems more like a teenager who claims to be on his own while secretly using his parents' credit card. In a world where states are constantly interconnected, the idea of absolute sovereignty is like a nostalgic daydream. The truth? Even the most proud nations today are dependent on international markets, multilateral organizations and technological developments. Sovereignty may exist on paper, but in practice it is often a matter of negotiation, a balancing act between national autonomy and global interdependence. Ironically, true strength is not in isolated self-determination but in how sovereign a state can cooperate with others.

The paradox of sovereignty in the modern world is that the very forces that enhance a nation's power, economic globalization, technological advancement and international cooperation, are also the same forces that challenge the traditional concept of sovereignty. While countries may still retain control over their borders and their institutions, they are inextricably bound to the global system in ways that limit their absolute control.

The thought that a country could make some sacrifices in its own power to strengthen the Union as a whole meets with as much resistance as a diet from someone who has eaten too much. Opposition to the EU is like a nightmare in which everything European is seen as a threat. Who wants consensus and cooperation when he can roll into the true depths of nationalism and hostile images of bygone eras?

There's nothing more romantic than the struggle for national sovereignty, that magical land where the leader alone decides what's good for the country and there's no outside influence, except perhaps from the international corporations that already control everything. The idea that a country could make sacrifices of its own accord to strengthen the union as a whole meets with as much resistance as feeding a person who has eaten too much. Resistance to the EU is like a nightmare in which everything European is perceived as a threat. Who wants consensus and cooperation when they can drift into the true depths of nationalism and hostility? There can be no determination when fear stands in the way.

The fear of political reactions, economic losses or

geopolitical consequences paralyses decision-making and prevents leaders from taking bold, clear action. The fear of escalation, as in dealing with Russia, the fear of internal tensions, are all these issues where hesitation, avoidance or willingness to compromise seem the safer way.

But when fear is at the forefront, true determination cannot be developed. Decisions are then made not from a position of strength, but from a position of uncertainty and hesitation. And that's when the illusion of union arises. It seems big and powerful, but it is so imbued with fear that it loses its own ability to act.The fear of escalation, such as in the context of the Ukraine conflict, takes diplomacy to an unreal level.

Additionally, the fear of one's own member states, which are guided by national interests in every decision, paralyzes the Union as a whole. Fear leads to the future and potential consequences always taking precedence in urgent decisions, such as those regarding a common

European defense policy or a coherent migration strategy.

Yet the future becomes increasingly unclear, when nobody takes decisive and bold stances in the present. If a Union is unable to overcome its fears and to take a determined position, it becomes a political field of contradictions. We then see a Europe that remains active on many fronts but never truly takes control, out of fear of the reactions that each decision might bring.

Courage is necessary to overcome fear. And courage is what can help overcome hesitation in critical moments. Europe must decide whether to let itself be paralyzed by fear or muster the courage to take responsibility and steer towards a determined future. Perhaps Orbán is not the true obstacle to Europe's determination. The real challenge may lie in a collective lack of courage, which stems from a deeply rooted fear of nuclear escalation. The intimidation tactics through nuclear threats act on some European decision-makers like an invisible but extremely effective barrier. They not only paralyze political discussions but also prevent clear, determined actions.

The decision-making weakness in Chancellor Scholz's leadership may be related to this psychological phenomenon, linked to a kind of conditioned fear or misperception of the threat. His avoidance strategy, hesitating and avoiding to prevent larger conflicts, is not necessarily the result of weakness in the traditional sense, but rather a response to the psycho-political pressure created by the perceived threat of war and global power plays, which weak characters cannot withstand. In a sense, it reflects the self-preservation logic, which, in the hope of avoiding evil, ends up encouraging inaction in practice.

What is the cowardice of an oversaturated society? How can such a cowardly, destructive attitude be prevented from emerging in future generations? In a satiated society, many live blindly in their familiar environment and have little incentive to take risks or push for change. The loss of comfort is often perceived as a threat, which doesn't stop people from clinging to the status quo. Society often lives in a state of convenience, which lulls it into a false sense of security. In such cases, people become so focused on their own concerns that they fail to realize how fragile these freedoms really are. Even political decision-makers, who should be the guardians of this freedom, sometimes seem distracted by short-term interests or populist currents. The focus shifts from actually securing freedom to power politics, short-term gain, or eyeing the next election.

It's almost as if society falls into a sort of sleep, while the foundations of liberty, freedom of speech, pluralism and equality are gradually under attack. The day may come when one realizes that the seemingly self-evident values are no longer so self-evident. The tragic part is that many won't notice this development until it's too late, or when the political landscape has shifted so much that the erosion of liberty can no longer be recognized as such. Therefore, a kind of awakening of society is needed, an awareness of the valuable treasure we carry in liberty. And the more people and decision-makers understand this, the better we will be equipped to face the challenges of the future without giving up our freedom.Passivity can be considered cowardice because it reduces the willingness to face uncomfortable truths, difficult decisions, or the need for change.

In times of abundance, people are more likely to stay in their comfortable little microcosm instead of engaging in social or political discourse. In such a society, fear of change spreads. The status quo, though perhaps imperfect, is considered safe and any form of change is seen as a threat. This attitude then turns into deeper destructiveness when society collectively adopts a passive stance that prevents it from enacting necessary changes.

The fear of Evil in International Politics must not extinguish hope. In an era where global headlines are often dominated by conflict, authoritarianism and humanitarian crises, it is easy, and even tempting, for fear to take precedence over hope. From war-torn regions to rising tensions between global powers, the specter of evil seems ever-present in the arena of international politics. Yet, while fear is a natural response to violence and injustice, it must never be allowed to overshadow hope. In fact, hope is not just a moral imperative, it is a strategic necessity.

International politics has always operated under the shadow of fear. fear of invasion, of ideological domination, of economic collapse. The Cold War was built on the premise of mutual suspicion, and today's geopolitical dynamics often mirror that zero-sum mentality. In such a climate, leaders may justify aggression, surveillance, or repression as necessary tools of security. Populations, too, may become susceptible to nationalist rhetoric or isolationist policies, driven by fear of the other. While fear might offer temporary control or unity, it is inherently corrosive. It narrows vision, erodes trust, and can lead to cycles of escalation. When international decisions are based primarily on worst-case scenarios, the capacity to envision cooperative, peaceful outcomes diminishes.

Hope in international politics is not naïve idealism, it is an act of strategic imagination. It allows to negotiate treaties, activists to fight for justice and nations to rebuild after conflict. Hope is what powered the formation of the United Nations after World War II, the peaceful fall of the Berlin Wall and global initiatives like the Paris Climate Agreement. When hope is present, it opens the door for diplomacy, innovation and collective action. It shifts the question from "How do we defend ourselves?" to "How do we build together?" In doing so, it enables solutions that are more sustainable, inclusive and morally grounded. If fear is allowed to fully extinguish hope, international politics devolves into pure survivalism. Multilateralism breaks down. Human rights are trampled in the name of national security. Climate action is stalled by short-term interests. Despair breeds apathy, or worse, extremism.

To be hopeful in the face of evil is not to deny the presence of danger, it is to reject its inevitability. This distinction is vital in an age where crises, whether political, social, environmental, or moral seem to multiply without end. Fear is a natural response to such realities. It warns us, protects us and forces us to recognize threats. But when fear becomes dominant, it paralyzes. It whispers that nothing can be done, that change is futile, and that resistance is meaningless. Hope stands in direct defiance of that voice.

Contrary to popular belief, hope is not the luxury of the naive. It is not a soft emotion reserved for idealists. True hope is disciplined, conscious and often forged in the harshest conditions. It demands clarity, not delusion. It sees the full weight of suffering and still chooses to act. In this sense, hope is not passive belief but active resistance. It is the belief that human action still matters even in the darkest circumstances, that injustice, no matter how entrenched, can be challenged, that compassion can still outlive cruelty.

History confirms this. Whether in the fall of oppressive regimes, the slow victories of civil rights movements, or the endurance of individuals who refuse to give up their dignity under persecution. Progress has never come from those who surrendered to fear, but from those who chose hope as their weapon. Hope is also strategic. A society that loses hope loses not only its moral compass but also its capacity for action. Without hope, there is no reason to participate, to protest, to vote, or to dream. Hopelessness breeds apathy, and apathy sustains the status quo.

This is why hope must be taught, protected and practiced, especially by the next generation. We must raise young people not just to see the world as it is, but to imagine what it could be. We must show them that fear is not an excuse to retreat, and that comfort is not a substitute for conscience. If we fail to do this, we risk raising a generation that sees evil as inevitable and injustice as unchangeable. To hope, therefore, is not to close one's eyes to danger. It is to keep them wide open and still choose to move forward.

International politics must remain rooted in realism, but it must also dare to imagine progress. Fear may alert us to threats, but it is hope that will ultimately allow us to transcend them. The path forward requires courage: the courage to engage with adversaries, to invest in peace even when it seems distant, and to uphold human dignity even when it is inconvenient. In doing so, we affirm that the future of our world belongs not to those who spread fear, but to those who keep hope alive.

The younger generation needs to understand what resilience means and what it can achieve. It is about the ability to overcome setbacks and not be discouraged by adversity. A society that nurtures empathy and a strong sense of community is less likely to fall into destructive cowardice. When people see themselves as part of something larger, they are more likely to take responsibility and work for the well-being of the community.

In such a society, people are not isolated individuals but active participants in the social and cultural shaping. Taking responsibility means not only caring about one's own benefit but also keeping the well-being of others in mind and actively working for change. It's a healthy blend of resilience, empathy and a sense of belonging to a community that enables the younger generation to overcome the cowardice of an overly comfortable society.

What's needed is a kind of superhero team, where each person brings their own abilities, but all are on a mission together to save the well-being of the community. Instead of always chasing the perfect Instagram post, they think about the world outside and ask themselves how they can help. These community heroes show that each of them has the ability to make a difference. It's not just about having superpowers, but also about stepping up for the well-being of the community with empathy, creativity, and commitment.

At its core, fear in international politics is not just a reaction to tangible threats but also a psychological phenomenon. Leaders and policymakers are influenced by their perceptions of threats, which may not always align with objective reality. The concept of "security dilemmas" describes how one nation's actions to enhance its security, such as increasing military spending, can inadvertently make other nations feel less secure, leading to an arms race or escalation of tensions.

The fear of loss of power or influence, the fear of being left behind in a rapidly changing world and the fear of making wrong decisions under pressure can all cloud the judgment of political leaders. In some cases, these fears may lead to overly cautious behavior, which can hinder diplomatic efforts and prevent timely responses to crises. In other cases, these fears may result in aggressive actions based on exaggerated perceptions of threat.

Fear remains one of the most significant factors in shaping international politics. While fear can sometimes drive positive action, such as the creation of international agreements or military alliances, more often, it leads to reactive and defensive policies that perpetuate insecurity. In the future, global leaders will need to find ways to manage and mitigate fear more effectively, addressing the root causes of insecurity and fostering cooperation in a rapidly changing world.

Ultimately, overcoming fear in international politics will require a combination of strategic foresight, diplomacy and collaboration. By addressing the psychological and material sources of fear, countries can work toward a more stable, secure, and cooperative global system. In international politics, it seems as if we are constantly in a game of fear, a bit like a scary thriller in which each actor is anxious to outsmart the others. But in fact the solution could be so simple: strategic foresight, diplomacy and cooperation! Who would have thought that deciphering the secrets of global security could be so simple?

By tackling the psychological and material sources of fear, countries could actually start to create a more stable and secure world. Maybe we should just offer the diplomats some meditation classes or call for an international "cuddle", a little less mistrust and a bit more team spirit! After all, if we all work together, the world could not only become safer, but perhaps also a little less dramatic. Who knows, maybe the next big international meeting will be not only about negotiations but also about a sense of community. Irony aside, the prospect of a cooperative global future is certainly a goal worth pursuing.

15. WHERE DO THE MEDIA STANDIN ALLIANCE?

There are plenty of them, the would-be analysts with little solid training. There are fewer brilliant analysts, but they do exist. The media landscape is in a state of upheaval, a mixture of information overload and echo chambers that makes it increasingly difficult to distinguish between real knowledge and superficial speculation. The many would-be analysts like to cavort on social media or give their opinions in mass publications without having a sound education or the in-depth expertise of a political, empirical or psychological nature that makes for sound analysis. These self-proclaimed experts have proliferated due to the democratization of information and the platforms of the digital age. They produce superficialities that are based more on sensationalism than on sound knowledge.

Why do the media companies get the madmen of journalism? Probably because they are cheap. They rely on sensationalism and quick, superficial reporting instead of providing in-depth and well-researched content. Tools such as artificial intelligence or automated news feeds are often used to produce news quickly and inexpensively. This lowers costs, but at the expense of quality and intellectual perspective. The editorial teams of many media houses have shrunk, resulting in fewer journalists and editors available for in-depth research and reporting. The workload is spread across fewer shoulders and quality suffers.

On the other hand, of course, there are the brilliant experts who offer truly in-depth insights into complex political, economic and social phenomena. However, these experts tend to be a rare breed in a media world that is increasingly fast-paced, clickbait-driven and often focused on short-term attention. It takes a lot of patience and expertise to get through to the real experts. It's difficult because the complexity of the issues is often distorted by the constant demand for simplified, accessible explanations.

The media industry has changed dramatically, and the competition for attention has even brought manipulative analysis to the fore. In this flood of information, how can we ensure that the voices of true experts and brilliant analysts are not lost in the noise? The challenge for the media lies not only in disseminating information, but also in distinguishing knowledge and wisdom from opinion and pseudo-knowledge.

In essence, it's a multi-faceted challenge that requires media outlets and audiences to be more discerning. By creating a system that values depth, expertise, and diversity of thought over immediacy and clickability, we can protect the integrity of informed analysis in a noisy world. This perspective highlights the importance of fostering a media landscape that prioritizes quality over quantity. To achieve this, media outlets can invest in rigorous investigative journalism, promote long-form content, and feature expert opinions that provide in-depth analysis. Audiences, on the other hand, can cultivate critical thinking skills, seek out reputable sources, and support platforms that emphasize thoughtful discourse.

Moreover, creating a culture that rewards well-researched articles and diverse viewpoints can help shift the focus away from sensationalism and towards meaningful engagement. By collectively advocating for a media ecosystem that values depth and insight, we can navigate the complexities of today's information overload and ensure that informed analysis remains a cornerstone of public discourse. Ultimately, this approach not only enhances our understanding of important issues but also strengthens democratic processes by encouraging informed participation.

This is precisely where the responsibility and relevance of think tanks and rating agencies come into play. They are the institutions of the future that claim to deliver high-quality analyses and objective assessments. Rating agencies of a completely different kind to financial market auditors have the task of assessing the political status of countries, actions and decision-makers. Financial vulnerability is also a major security risk.

Countries that have a high level of debt or lose their credit rating are more susceptible to economic and social crises. Not only does such a case bring down the quality of life of citizens, it also drives social unrest or even political instability as governments are forced to take drastic measures such as austerity programs or tax increases. Countries with weak financial systems are less able to invest in security and defense measures. This makes them more vulnerable to external threats, as their military or diplomatic capacity to act is limited.

Financial instability makes companies and states attractive targets for cybercrime and hacker attacks. Criminal organizations and hostile states are thus invited to focus on the destruction of financial systems or the manipulation of financial markets. Financial instability and the lack of investment in companies also lead to problems in global supply chains, jeopardizing economic security and the supply of essential goods. This affects not only the economy, but also local security, particularly in relation to critical infrastructure. Protecting financial stability is therefore just as important as protecting against military threats when it comes to ensuring a country's long-term security.

To mitigate risks and increase resilience, countries need to develop integrated strategies that address both financial and security challenges simultaneously. This includes, for example, promoting stable economic conditions, supporting institutions that focus on economic and security aspects, and creating crisis management mechanisms that incorporate both areas.

The press plays a crucial role in raising awareness of these interrelationships. However, the complex nuances are often not sufficiently identified or addressed. This can lead to the public receiving an incomplete picture of the challenges and the necessary measures. Well-founded reporting that highlights the interactions between financial and security policy is therefore of great importance in order to promote informed discussions and support political decision-makers.

Evaluation committees come into play. Their task is to create and maintain trust. In a world where political and economic interests often call the tune, these institutions must question their independence and integrity in an environment where skepticism about institutional evaluations is often on the rise. Their reputation is at stake if they are unable to maintain the distinction between independent analysis and opinion-driven discourse.

The free market could actually play a very important role in promoting the integrity of think tanks and rating agencies by providing a natural selective force. In a market where reliability and credibility are the basis for long-term success, these institutions must ensure that they actually fulfill their claim to objectivity. If they do not, there is a risk that they will be squeezed out by better, more transparent providers.

In an environment in which user expectations increasingly demand objective and precise information, only those that are credible and reliable will prevail in the long term. Rating agencies that provide accurate assessments and disclose their methodology, for example, could gain a clear advantage over less transparent providers. Think tanks that analyze independently and impartially and present these analyses clearly and comprehensibly have the opportunity to find a growing following among those looking for sound, fact-based insights.

The institutions that succeed in the long run will be those that place the highest value on transparency, independence, and clarity while providing evidence-backed, trustworthy information. Whether in the form of a rating agency or a think tank, establishing a reputation for credibility, reliability, and impartiality will set these entities apart in an increasingly competitive media environment. As users grow more sophisticated and discerning, these values will be crucial for attracting and maintaining a dedicated audience.

The market mechanisms also provide a feedback loop that enables a kind of self-regulation. If an institution such as a think tank or rating agency acts with blatant political or economic interests and questions its independence, this will be reflected relatively quickly in the market. In a world increasingly characterized by digital transparency and public debate, it is becoming increasingly difficult for such institutions to disguise opinion-driven discourse as qualitative analysis.

Competition in the free market can therefore indeed create a positive dynamic that helps to maintain trust in think tanks and rating agencies. If these institutions are able to maintain their independence, they will be able to gain trust and hold their own in an increasingly critical and skeptical environment. With a diverse array of institutions offering similar services, audiences are empowered to choose those that align with their values and needs. Think tanks and rating agencies that can prove their independence, back their claims with evidence, and provide thoughtful, thorough analyses are more likely to attract loyal audiences, ensuring that only those who earn trust thrive in the long term.

Competition in the free market fosters an environment in which quality, integrity, and credibility are rewarded, making it a vital force in building public trust in think tanks and rating agencies. In such a landscape, these agencies have a unique opportunity to distinguish themselves through rigorous, independent, and transparent analysis. However, to truly thrive, they must remain vigilant in safeguarding their institutional independence and methodological integrity. Analyses must be grounded in sound, replicable research and communicated with clarity and openness.

Those that succeed in cultivating a reputation for

reliable, fact-based insights will not only endure in an era of growing public scrutiny and skepticism, but will emerge as indispensable actors in shaping informed policy and public discourse. In this sense, trust is not granted, it is earned, continuously and deliberately, through a demonstrated commitment to truth over trend, and evidence over ideology.

In large alliances and multinational partnerships, the media play a particularly sensitive and complex role that goes beyond their traditional function of reporting news. They operate at the intersection of democratic accountability, public engagement, and cross-border understanding. Large alliances involve complex, multilayered decision-making processes that can be opaque to the public. The media's task is to shed light on these structures and make decisions comprehensible, especially when they are made at levels removed from national parliaments or direct democratic oversight. Without independent journalism, there is a high risk of a legitimacy gap, which can be easily exploited by populist or extremist narratives.

International alliances bring together diverse political cultures, priorities, and values. The media can foster a shared understanding of the alliance's purpose and challenges, helping to create a sense of cohesion. At the same time, they should not conceal tensions or disagreements but explain them constructively, contributing to a more nuanced and informed public discourse. Citizens often feel detached from the decision-making processes of large alliances, believing they have little say. Media can counteract this sense of alienation by stimulating democratic debate, highlighting voices from civil society, and making complex topics accessible. This helps ensure that these alliances remain anchored in democratic values and public support.

Alliances are frequent targets of disinformation campaigns, often orchestrated by authoritarian regimes or anti-democratic actors. Independent, professional media are a first line of defense in identifying, debunking, and contextualizing such narratives. Their ability to maintain public trust and protect the integrity of the information space is crucial for the resilience of democratic institutions.In doing so, they serve as both watchdogs and bridge-builders, ensuring that international cooperation remains rooted in transparency, accountability and public understanding.

16. ALLIANCES - ASSETS
OF THE GLOBAL FUTURE

Alliances are important assets of the global future on many overlapping levels. The world is becoming increasingly interconnected.. It will no longer be able to manage without alliances. Cooperation keeps it afloat. While national interests and isolated power structures may have dominated in the past, today it is interdependent networks and strategic partnerships that ensure success.

National solo efforts are becoming less effective, as many challenges such as security and freedom, climate change, pandemics and technological disruptions require global solutions. Strategic partnerships make it possible to pool resources, knowledge and technologies in order to drive innovation faster and more effectively. No single power has the capacity to solve all problems. Cooperation is therefore essential.

Different units have different strengths. By working together, they can pool their resources, knowledge and technologies. From climate change to the challenges of artificial intelligence, these are global issues and they need global solutions. And strategic partnerships minimize conflicts. Climate change is an excellent example of a global problem that can only be tackled through international cooperation. No single country can significantly reduce emissions, master the transition to renewable energy or overcome the effects of the climate crisis on its own. In this area, cooperation between states, international organizations, companies and NGOs is crucial.

Collaboration is also of central importance in the field of artificial intelligence. Developments in AI affect many areas of society, from the world of work and data protection to ethical and security issues. Coordinated, international cooperation in research and development, but also in regulation and the creation of ethical standards, is essential to ensure that AI is used responsibly and for the benefit of humanity as a whole. Strategic partnerships between governments, companies and scientific institutions play a key role in promoting innovation and minimizing risks.

Another very important element is that strategic partnerships can minimize conflicts. In geopolitically and economically tense times, cooperation offers an opportunity to reduce tensions and avoid conflict. By combining their strengths, be it in technology, economics or diplomacy, countries can contribute to a more stable and peaceful world order. Partnerships can also help to build mutual trust and promote common interests, rather than countries acting in isolation and potentially exacerbating conflict.

As alliances can foster exchanges between cultures and societies, they can also eliminate misunderstandings. A networked world is one that understands each other better. The global assets of the future are therefore to be found not only in commodities or money, but in the relationships that are forged. The winners are those who build such networks effectively, be it through technical innovation, crisis management or geopolitical stability.

Countries must position themselves in a fragmented global system and use strategic partnerships to safeguard their interests. At the same time, alliances offer opportunities for the middle and emerging countries to strengthen their geopolitical role. But also irritations are inevitable in any alliance. Sometimes they are the touchstones against which the strength and resilience of such a partnership is measured. The greatest disruptions occur when expectations are not met, values do not agree or interests come into conflict.

While alliances offer enormous potential for progress and collective strength, if even one wheel gets out of sync, it can bring the whole machine to a standstill. In a world where each part of a global alliance is intertwined, the failure of one partner, whether political, economic or social, will have far-reaching consequences. It's like in a clockwork, when a gear wheel jams or loosens, whole parts of the machinery are disabled.

If a member of an alliance suddenly experiences political turbulence or instability, be it through a change of government, conflict or ideological division, the entire cooperation will be at risk. An unstable partner immediately unsettles the whole common agenda. Take, for example, the geopolitical situation in certain regions where political upheavals in a country have an impact on neighbouring nations and even put international cooperation into turmoil.

Therefore, alliances should not only aim to benefit from the benefits of cooperation, but also focus on a strategy of resilience. This means that you develop mechanisms to maintain the alliance in the event of a spinning wheel. A certain degree of flexibility will be crucial. As soon as a partner is in crisis, the alliance should be able to adapt and continue working together in other ways or find alternative solutions. Alliances should not depend solely on a single partner. Diversifying relationships and resource allocation to several strong partners can help minimize the risk of failure by one partner not bringing down the entire alliance.

In alliances where partners rely too much on each other, overload can occur. A member feels pressured to deliver more and more while other partners withdraw or contribute less. This creates feelings of being exploited, resulting in frustration and resignation. It requires the willingness to recognize conflicts and find solutions together. An alliance should not only flourish in times of prosperity and success, but also when things are shaky.

Once irritation occurs, it is important not to ignore or hide the conflict. The ability to adapt to change and regularly review the alliance's goals helps keep an alliance on track in a constantly changing world. So irritations are not necessarily the end of an alliance, but a chance to deepen and strengthen cooperation. If they are seen as a test of resilience and an opportunity for improvement, such grains of sand in machinery can play a crucial role in making an alliance successful in the long term.

A global alliance can play a transformative role in the geopolitical and economic landscape. It could pave the way for a specific era of international cooperation, innovation and sustainable development by uniting the strengths and common interests of these countries in a dynamic alliance. Such an alliance would, however, have to pursue a common vision and clear strategies that encourage effective cooperation, internally and externally. This alliance could serve as a solid cooperative structure.

A large-scale alliance can act as a security architecture, using its collective strength, shared values and geostrategic reach to deter aggression, prevent large-scale conflicts and promote international stability. By coordinating defense capabilities, intelligence-sharing, and diplomatic influence, such an alliance not only protects its member states but also contributes to the broader international order. Beyond deterrence, a well-structured alliance must also invest in conflict prevention and resolution mechanisms. This includes early-warning systems, crisis diplomacy, peacekeeping capacities and partnerships with regional actors. In doing so, it positions itself not merely as a military bloc, but as a force for peace, stability and multilateral problem-solving. In a world marked by growing polarization, authoritarian resurgence and hybrid threats, the ability of an alliance to act proactively, not just reactively, will determine its relevance. Security today is no longer only about borders, it is about values, resilience and the capacity to mediate in a complex, interconnected world.

India, for example, which plays a key role in the Indo-Pacific, could play also an important role in peacekeeping in close cooperation with Europe and Canada. Particularly on security issues such as counterterrorism and securing international sea routes, member states could work together to pool their political and military influence.

Another central element would be the promotion of world trade and economic cooperation. This strategy could be supported by the promotion of sustainable development and a completely different kind of financial cooperation. Members oft he Pact would stabilize their financial markets and support sustainable financing models based on environmentally friendly infrastructure and a military security concept.

Through an increasingly open and fair world trade, a multilateral world order might be able to secure global peace and economic stability. The alliance would function as a peace and security architecture that takes into account the situation of member states and jointly assumes responsibility for international stability. The alliance could deepen cooperation in the areas of counter-terrorism, securing international sea routes and peace missions.

India is an emerging power in the Indo-Pacific region. It

could also serve as a diplomatic bridge between the Near East and the Middle East. Europe, for its part, could benefit from a military and security cooperation to secure its own eastern flank while acting as a link between the Atlantic and the Indo-Pacific. An expanded exchange in the area of military security, particularly in areas such as cyber security, counter-terrorism and the security of global air and sea routes, would affect the interests of all parties involved.

In a new alliance, India would have the chance to free itself from the pretext of a conditioned fata-morgana in global affairs. After all, India has the highest economic growth rate in the world at 6-7%. Although it is a leader in many sectors such as IT, aerospace and pharmaceuticals, there are still deep social and economic disparities that are reflected in widespread poverty and unequal opportunities for different population groups. India faces a number of challenges that are also present in other emerging countries. It has to tackle environmental problems such as air pollution and water shortages, promoting the education sector and healthcare and creating jobs for the young, rapidly growing population. Taking a significant position in a new global alliance could fundamentally change it. Nevertheless, given the discrepancies between the parts of a high-performance society and the rest of a population still stigmatized by poverty, seeing India as a soon-to-be world power is a clear overestimation. Outdated ideas could soon be realigned. The joint creation of a new alliance would make India and the other members a global power.

On another platform, Eastern European countries been increasingly focused on modernizing their defense sectors due to growing security concerns. India, with its strong defense industry, which includes advanced military technologies and systems, could be a valuable partner in addressing these needs. This collaboration might extend beyond just arms sales, encompassing joint R&D, technology transfers, and shared military exercises. As Eastern Europe looks to diversify their defense relationships, India's role as a non-Western, non-Russian power could present a balanced alternative.

On the other hand, India's space program has grown significantly, making it a key player in the global space race. Cooperation with Europe, where space technology and research are highly advanced space industries, would be a natural and promising area of collaboration. Moreover, India could offer an affordable and highly efficient solution to European countries seeking cost-effective space launch services. In return, India could gain access to more advanced space technologies, satellite communications, and joint scientific research, which would accelerate the growth of its own space sector.

With Europe, India could boost its geopolitical influence in the region, offering an alternative to reliance on Russia or the U.S., while also gaining access to strategic defense technologies and new markets for its defense exports. India could advance its ambitions in space exploration independently of the major powers, while also benefiting from scientific collaboration and expanding its role as a partner in global technological advancements.

A fair and open trade environment should promote environmentally friendly and green technologies. Europe would benefit from increased economic cooperation with emerging economies such as India and the Middle East. This would also strengthen Europe's economic structure, especially with regard to new markets and technologies.

Europe and India have a significant responsibility for global development. Given their different historical and geopolitical backgrounds, but also their growing importance in the global economy and politics, a joint roadmap to promote sustainable global development could make perfect sense. And there are several areas in which such a cooperation could be concretized.
Europe as well as India have a strong common interest in

combating climate change and promoting sustainable development. Europe has a long tradition in environmental policy and can offer valuable experience in the implementation of green technologies, sustainable agriculture and renewable energy. In turn, India has much to offer when it comes to cost-effective solutions and innovation in sustainable infrastructure, as it is under immense pressure to develop sustainable development strategies due to its large population and growth momentum.

In the realm of technology, particularly in the fields of artificial intelligence, digitalization and space exploration, a new alliance could forge a robust partnership that harnesses the strengths of diverse regions. To facilitate a technology-driven collaboration among Europe, Canada, India, and East Asia a well-structured roadmap would be essential. It should prioritize the exchange of knowledge and technologies, fostering an environment where innovation can thrive across borders. By establishing joint research programs, participants can leverage their unique expertise and resources, tackling pressing challenges that span economic and social dimensions. For instance, initiatives could be launched to address critical issues such as digital literacy and accessibility, ensuring that marginalized communities are not left behind in the digital revolution.

For countries such as South Korea and Canada, participation in a forward-looking international alliance presents not only geopolitical advantages but also significant economic and technological opportunities. Such an alliance could serve as a catalyst for access to new markets, innovation networks, and strategic partnerships, particularly in the rapidly evolving fields of future-oriented technologies. Joint efforts in areas such as artificial intelligence, quantum computing, blockchain, green energy, and digital infrastructure are more than just symbolic gestures of cooperation, they represent critical investments in global competitiveness. By pooling resources, talent and technological expertise, member states can accelerate breakthroughs that might be unattainable in isolation. This collective approach enables smaller but highly capable nations like Canada and South Korea to punch above their weight on the global tech stage.

One area of particular promise is the cross-border development of innovation ecosystems. This includes the exchange of researchers and students, the co-founding of start-ups, and the creation of joint research centers or innovation labs. These institutions can serve as nodes in a wider innovation network, facilitating not only the sharing of knowledge and infrastructure but also fostering cultural understanding and trust among next-generation leaders.

Furthermore, such cooperation enhances economic resilience. By diversifying technological supply chains and reducing dependency on authoritarian regimes or single-source suppliers, allied democracies can better safeguard both their strategic autonomy and the integrity of their digital economies. Finally, by anchoring technological advancement in shared democratic values, such alliances help shape the global governance of emerging technologies, ensuring that innovation serves not just markets, but societal well-being, transparency, and human rights.

Given that the countries in question, such as South Korea, Canada and other like-minded democracies,place a high priority on geopolitical stability and national security, a future-oriented alliance should aim to build a balanced and robust security network. This network would go beyond bilateral defense ties and evolve into a strategic, multilayered security framework, capable of addressing conventional threats and hybrid challenges in an increasingly unpredictable global environment.

Such an alliance should be anchored in coordinated defense cooperation, intelligence sharing, and joint military readiness, allowing member states to act swiftly and collectively in times of crisis. Crucially, it must be flexible and adaptive, able to respond to emerging threats such as cyberattacks, disinformation campaigns, and disruptions to critical infrastructure. To consolidate peace and promote regional stability, the alliance should establish and strengthen geostrategic security agreements in key global flashpoints, most notably the Indo-Pacific region, the Middle East, and Europe's eastern flank. These regions are not only central to global trade and energy flows but also hotspots for geopolitical tension and power competition. Through joint military exercises, regional security dialogues, capacity-building programs, and support for democratic institutions, the alliance can act as a stabilizing force.

Moreover, the alliance could create innovation networks that connect startups and established enterprises, fostering collaboration and knowledge sharing. These networks would not only stimulate economic growth but also encourage the development of solutions aimed at societal challenges, such as climate change, public health, and equitable access to technology. In essence, this partnership has the potential to create a comprehensive ecosystem that promotes sustainable technological advancement while addressing the broader implications of digital transformation. By working together, these regions can not only enhance their individual capabilities but also contribute to a more interconnected and resilient global community. This proactive approach will ensure that the benefits of technology are shared widely, paving the way for a future that is inclusive and equitable for all.

Europe, with its strong institutional frameworks, deep expertise in regulatory affairs and extensive experience in fostering international collaborations, is well-positioned to play a pivotal role in coordinating and managing such a technology-driven alliance. Europe has a long history of establishing successful multi-country collaborations, such as the European Union itself and various European research initiatives, e.g., Horizon Europe. Building on this experience, Europe could spearhead the creation of governance frameworks for the alliance. This would involve defining clear roles, responsibilities, and decision-making processes, ensuring that all participants have a fair say and that the collaboration remains transparent and effective. By setting up a central coordinating body or steering committee composed of representatives from each partner region, Europe could ensure smooth management and alignment of goals. This body could be responsible for setting long-term strategic priorities, allocating funding, and overseeing the progress of joint research programs and technological initiatives.

Europe is home to numerous leading research institutions, universities and technology companies. Leveraging this knowledge base, Europe could act as a facilitator for the exchange of ideas, research, and technology between the alliance's partners. Europe could also leverage its experience in digital policies and ethical standards for emerging technologies. By coordinating discussions around regulatory frameworks for AI ethics, data privacy, and digital governance, Europe can ensure that the alliance's technological developments are aligned with global standards and best practices, promoting responsible innovation across regions. Providing a framework for cross-border collaboration, Europe could help facilitate the creation of shared innovation hubs where scientists, technologists, and entrepreneurs can come together to tackle issues like digital literacy, climate change and public health. These hubs could also serve as incubators for startups and small enterprises, supporting them through mentorship, funding and access to international markets. Europe could act as a mediator, connecting key stakeholders from the public as well as from the private sectors across all four regions. Europe has been at the forefront of advocating for sustainable development goals and ethical technology. This perspective could shape the alliance's approach to technology development, ensuring that the alliance's projects align with global goals related to sustainability, social inclusion, and climate resilience.

On the other side of global developments that take into account the demands of the major powers, strategic alliances are forming between Russia, China, Iran and North Korea. Their goal is to challenge the existing world order and create a new one that corresponds to their own political, economic and security objectives. They promote authoritarian values, seek to marginalize human rights and work to shift global power dynamics in their favor. Furthermore, China's methods are often described as harsh. State-owned enterprises, coupled with advanced technologies like AI, surveillance cameras and modern high-tech tools of control, are employed to enforce strict societal control not only within China but also potentially in other countries. This use of technology, including tools of repression, points to a strategy that seeks absolute control over its own population and may extend its influence in ways that challenge individual freedoms globally. The technologies developed by state-owned companies are part of a larger set of high-tech violence tools used in authoritarian regimes to monitor, manipulate and suppress society.

When combined with AI, these technologies can track and analyze people's movements in public spaces, often without their knowledge or consent. In China, this is frequently used to monitor political dissidents or social movements. In authoritarian states, these technologies are used to suppress political resistance. There are reports that such technologies are also employed in repressive measures, such as targeting ethnic minorities. Another example of the use of such technologies is China's Social Credit System, which relies on surveillance technology and data analytics to monitor and rate citizens' behavior. Negative ratings can lead to restrictions on freedom of movement or access to certain services. China also exports these technologies to other countries, which can enhance its influence on global surveillance and control standards. Some of these technologies are also used in authoritarian regimes outside of China, raising concerns about their role in global social control.

The free democratic world often voices loud criticism, acts with restraint and remains internally divided when it comes to responding to authoritarian strategies. At best, small counter-movements emerge, at worst, the free world becomes a mere spectator in the global race for freedom and human rights. The free world is capable of more, but it must decide whether it truly wants to act. Without courage, clear values, and a shared strategy, it risks becoming not only a bystander, but perhaps soon an imitator of the authoritarian model.

The format of a global alliance as a counterpart would create an interesting new dynamic in international politics and economics. The free world is capable of far more, but it must decide whether it truly has the will to act. Without the courage to stand firm, a clear commitment to democratic values and a coherent, forward-looking strategy, liberal democracies risk becoming not only passive bystanders, but eventually, reluctant imitators of the authoritarian systems they once opposed. As authoritarian regimes grow bolder and more coordinated, the absence of unity and resolve among open societies sends a dangerous signal, that freedom can be negotiated and principles compromised for short-term convenience.

More than a symbolic gesture, this kind of alliance could become a structural pillar of 21st-century geopolitics, capable of countering coercive diplomacy, defending democratic norms and offering resilient alternatives to nations caught between competing models of governance. In doing so, it would reaffirm that democracy is not only worth defending, but still capable of shaping the future.

Imagine how the US, China and Russia would react. It's not hard to imagine that all three powers would be a little nervous about such an alliance. While these countries, with their own interests and ambitions, are determined to dominate the geopolitical chessboard, an alliance of India, South Korea, Canada, evenually the UAE and Europe could shake up their established majorities.

The US would probably be the first to come between concern and opportunistic curiosity. On the one hand, they have close relations with Canada and Europe, on the other hand, they might wonder whether this alliance does not turn the global trade order upside down, which they actually want to determine themselves. The US relies on its ability to play in alliances while seeking its own advantage. Washington would see the newly emerging alliance as a challenge and at the same time as an impetus to optimize its own trade relations and security strategies. Are they in the international orchestra or do they prefer to remain solitary alpha animals?

The reaction on China's side would be sharper. A united global alliance could weaken China's influence in Asia and Africa. So it would not be surprising if Beijing first tried to gauge its own reactions in terms of power and strength. At the same time, it would try to divide the countries within the alliance in order to prevent them from fully cooperating. An alliance is nice, but wait until China reveals its ambitions.

China would likely perceive such an alliance as a direct attempt to contain its rise and limit its global influence. The South China Sea, the Taiwan Strait and the border regions with India could see a growing military presence of China. China could also step up military exercises with allies like Russia or provide military support to strategic partners in exchange for the reinforcement of rights or political orientation.

This makes it all the more critical for the democratic world to respond, not with naïve escalation, but with firm, coordinated and value-driven resolve. Strategic clarity, not strategic hesitation, must shape the response. Democracies must demonstrate that deterrence is not provocation, and that defending freedom, sovereignty, and open societies is not a choice, but a necessity. A credible alliance of democracies must therefore be geopolitically prepared, diplomatically united, and technologically resilient, capable of withstanding pressure and actively shaping the rules of global engagement. Anything less would leave the field open to authoritarian expansion and a dangerous erosion of the international order.

China's ambitions have become more apparent, particularly in areas like economic influence, technological development, and military expansion. The globalized world has generally benefited from open markets, international cooperation and shared institutions, but China's vision of the future could push for a more centralized model where its own values and interests take precedence. Its growing influence in international organizations, control over key infrastructure projects like ports or telecommunications networks and policies in the South China Sea, all point to a desire to shape global norms to better fit its model. If China's ambitions unfold in a dramatic way, it could significantly alter the current global order, especially with how intertwined economies and political systems are today. For many countries, China's rise represents a shift away from the international system, with implications for trade, military alliances and even cultural influence.

Russia, for its part, would be immediately skeptical and suspicious of such an alliance, especially of the role of Europe and the UAE. Russia has deep geopolitical interests in Central Asia and the Middle East, which could potentially be threatened by the integration of the UAE and the increased role of South Korea and India. Russia could turn away from the strong hand mentality or try to slip into the gap between these countries by offering itself as a mediator or partner to destabilize the alliance.

The Kremlin, already allied with China on many fronts, would likely adopt an openly antagonistic stance.It would seek to undermine the alliance through asymmetric warfare. It is expected that disinformation campaigns, election manipulation and cyber attacks will increase. They could aim to sow discord within the "APTO" bloc, especially against the more vulnerable or divided democracies. Russia would further inflame conflicts in regions like the Middle East, the Balkans or Africa, where Western influence is limited, supporting regimes and groups opposed to APTO interests. Russia might deepen military ties with China, sharing arms technologies and conducting joint naval or nuclear exercises, signaling a hardening of a Eurasian authoritarian axis.

Iran would double down on its relationships with non-state actors like Hezbollah, the Houthis, and Shiite militias across the Middle East to counter Western and APTO-aligned Gulf states. This network of proxy forces serves as a key instrument for Tehran to project power and counterbalance the influence of Western-backed and APTO-aligned Gulf states.

The emergence of a powerful „APTO" alliance would not

go unanswered. The response from authoritarian powers would be swift and multifaceted, seeking to delegitimize, destabilize, and counterbalance the democratic bloc. We could witness the formation of a new geopolitical Cold War, not just in terms of military standoff, but in technological standards, trade routes, political ideology and influence over the Global South.

However, the international community must not give in. In the face of rising authoritarian assertiveness, the strength of freedom, democracy and human dignity must prevail. This means standing firm on universal values, defending open societies and investing in resilient partnerships. Freedom is not just a principle, it is a strategic asset. When democracies work together with determination, unity and purpose, they can withstand pressure, inspire others and offer a compelling alternative to coercion and control. The global balance of power may be shifting, but the moral and political strength of free societies must remain unwavering. This underscores the need for a coordinated regional and global response, one that combines military deterrence, strategic diplomacy and intelligence cooperation. If left unchecked, Iran's asymmetric approach could undermine broader efforts to stabilize the Middle East and maintain a rules-based regional order.

In today's world, technology is a battleground. The free world must prioritize cybersecurity, artificial intelligence ethics and information warfare to counter China's technological dominance and Russia's disinformation campaigns. It is equally vital to provide support for media outlets and civil society organizations in authoritarian states to combat the spread of state-controlled narratives.

While diplomacy and economic tools are essential, military deterrence remains a fundamental aspect of countering authoritarian aggression. The free world must ensure that defense commitments are maintained, particularly in Europe and the Indo-Pacific, to counter

Russia and China's expansionist tendencies. Moreover, building regional security arrangement, such as through partnerships with the Gulf states to combat Iranian proxies, will help diminish the strategic leverage of authoritarian regimes.

The free world's response must not solely be reactive, it must proactively promote the values of democracy and human rights. This involves not only condemning human rights violations in places like Xinjiang, Crimea, and Tehran but also supporting civil society in these regions. The international community should fund initiatives that strengthen democratic institutions, support free press, and protect the rights of minorities and dissidents.

By uniting across borders, economies, and ideologies, the free world has the potential to maintain its leadership in the face of these authoritarian challenges. But time is of the essence. Without a cohesive, bold response, the democratic world risks losing ground in a global struggle for values, freedom, and security.

In theory, pacts can be strong. Democracy, with all its values, could undoubtedly emerge victorious in a global struggle for freedom and security. But only if it avoids the endless debate about what an alliance should even be. And what happens if the alliance doesn't act fast enough? Well, it's simple, then it's their own fault. Who would have thought that defending good old idealism would ever be so hard. But instead of pointing fingers at the authoritarian regimes that are racing ahead of us in this power struggle, we're doing what we do best: explaining at length how great it would be to take the lead. The only thing growing faster than the challenge itself is the collection of consulting reports and white papers. Meanwhile, Russia celebrates another victory in Ukraine, China marches unhindered toward Taiwan and Iran continues to expand its regional power base. Who would have thought that a Free World would transform into a club whose members are drifting so far apart that they are only observing the threat from afar and arguing over who should make the first move? The truth is bitter. If we don't agree and act, then we're doing exactly what these authoritarian regimes wanted from the start, losing ourselves in an endless civilized dialogue. And while we continue to debate ourselves to death, the rest of the world slips away, and maybe, eventually, so will we. So, dear Alliance, it's time to act. Or it's your own fault.

17. THE FINANCIAL POWER
OF A GLOBAL ALLIANCE

In today's interconnected and politically sensitive global economy, capital allocation is not merely a financial decision, it is a strategic and ethical act. Where capital flows reflects not only the priorities of management but also the values of institutions and societies. Rational management must recognize that the decision of where to invest is inherently a decision about what kind of future we are financing. In this context, cooperation management must operate on multiple levels. First, it must evaluate financial returns and risks in the conventional sense - market potential, technological competitiveness, regulatory stability. But second, and increasingly crucial, is the evaluation of non-financial risks. reputation, regulatory sanctions and long-term alignment with stakeholder values, including environmental, social and governance concerns.

When ethical arguments are not enough, economic incentives and risks must be brought to the table. If decision-makers are not particularly interested in human rights, there is still one point of contact that always gets their attention: the cost-benefit calculation. As soon as that equation shifts, they start to listen. That's where politics, business, and diplomacy need to engage and it works. Human rights do have a lobby. It's called economy.

Those who want to make an impact in political or economic spheres must start exactly here. Human rights are often dismissed as a soft topic, an ideal fit for Sunday speeches. But in reality, they are a strategic factor with tangible consequences for supply chains, investment risks, international reputation and long-term market stability. Human rights violations lead to sanctions, consumer boycotts, brand damage, and legal challenges and that hits companies and governments where it hurts: at the economic core. Anyone who wants stable markets needs the rule of law. Anyone who seeks to foster innovation must protect freedom of expression. And those who aim to cooperate globally must respect fundamental rights. Those who combine ethics with efficiency can spark change that endures.

When ethical arguments are not enough, economic incentives and risks must be brought up. When decision-makers are not particularly interested in human rights, there is still an interface that they touch. As soon as the cost-benefit calculation starts, they become audible. So there has to be a place in politics, economy and diplomacy and that works. Anyone who wants to achieve impact in politics, economics or diplomacy must start right here. Human rights are often seen as a soft topic, an ideal for sunday speeches. But in reality they are a strategic factor with concrete effects on supply chains, investment risks, international reputation and long-term market stability. Human rights violations lead to sanctions, consumer boycotts, brand losses, legal actions and this hits companies and states where it hurts: on the economic nerve. Those who want stable markets need the rule of law and those who want to promote freedom of innovation must protect freedom of expression. And if you want to cooperate globally, you have to respect fundamental rights; if you combine ethics and efficiency, you can initiate changes that last.

Capital allocation is where corporate strategy meets moral responsibility. It is where management decides not just what is profitable, but what is permissible. This responsibility is heightened in an era where authoritarian regimes leverage advanced technologies to entrench control, and where international markets, often under the banner of innovation and digital transformation, serve as conduits for these technologies to proliferate globally.

As an example, when companies or institutional investors, allocate capital to firms like Tiandy in China, they do more than support technological development they help normalize and export models of digital authoritarianism. Conversely, choosing not to invest or to divest is a powerful signal. a declaration that profit cannot come at the expense of human dignity and international norms.

Further improvement of the euro's role in the global monetary system could bring far-reaching benefits to the new alliance, financially and geopolitically. A stronger role for the euro would help reduce the risk of dependence on other major currencies such as the US dollar. Especially in times of crisis, this could provide the countries and institutions of the Alliance with more stability and independence. This would strengthen economic stability and give the members of the alliance more control over their own financial markets. It could also make the companies from the alliance more competitive, as they could get better terms in international trade.

A euro that is more widely accepted worldwide will be perceived as an alternative source of finance and anchor of stability in an increasingly multipolar international system. Markets such as Indonesia and the Mercosur countries offer significant growth potential. These countries are experiencing high growth rates and are becoming important players in international trade. The development of trade agreements could improve access to these markets. Issuing bonds or forming a stable credit system could enable the alliance to access capital markets and manage its financial resources flexibly and effectively.

The question is how the Alliance implements the necessary reforms and strategies to bring the euro into such a position. A coherent and common policy within the Alliance would strengthen confidence in the euro. The alliance could also support the development of digital currencies and innovative financial technologies that promote the euro as a means of payment and increase its use in the digital economy. The Alliance should create incentives to establish the euro as a means of payment for international trade contracts. The euro could gain liquidity by expanding currency swap agreements with other major central banks such as the Bank of Japan, the Bank of Canada, the Bank of India or the Central Bank of United Arab Emirates. This would increase the availability of the euro in the international financial system and at the same time provide an inexhaustible source of financing for innovations that are crucial to increasing productivity and growth.

The financial strength of a global alliance is central to its success and long-term stability, especially if it is to be able to influence the international economic space and safeguard its own interests. A strong financial base enables not only economic influence, but also geopolitical power. A prominent position of the euro in the global financial system would provide an alliance with a solid basis for international trade and financial transactions. This improves the alliance's financial autonomy by relying less on the US dollar.

The People's Republic of China has long speculated with

a counter-part. China has been working hard in recent years to establish the yuan as an alternative currency to reduce dependence on the US dollar. A crucial step was the inclusion of the yuan in the currency basket of the International Monetary Fund as official reserve currency in 2016. This decision made the yuan an important currency in the international trade and global financial markets.

China's strategy includes promoting the Chinese yuan as a global reserve currency and diversifying international trade relations and financial instruments. China has also tried to position the yuan more strongly in global oil trade, especially with the introduction of yuan-denominated oil futures. If countries trade oil in yuan instead of US dollars, this could lead to a shift towards a bipolarity of the global reserve currencies dollar and yuan.

In addition, Chinese banks offer loans in yuan, which helps to displace the dollar in the affected regions and promote the global use of the yuan. China has bilateral currency agreements with many countries where trade is conducted directly in national currencies or yuan, rather than using the US dollar as an intermediate currency. This helps to further reduce the role of the US dollar in international trade and increase international demand for the yuan. Such a financial hegemonic position cannot please everyone. For the US, losing the dollar as a global reserve currency would mean that it would have less control over international capital flows and could no longer finance its trade deficits so easily.

Since the yuan is subject to strict domestic capital controls, the Chinese government has a significant influence on how the yuan is traded and used in international markets. This form of control could deter international actors who prefer greater currency freedom. The yuan, despite its increasing international use, is highly susceptible to political intervention and market volatility. For many countries, the yuan is therefore less attractive because it does not offer the same flexibility as the dollar or the euro.

The topic of dedollarization has become an important point in Chinese economic policy in recent years. Dedollarization refers to the process of reducing dependence on the US dollar in international trade and financial transactions. China has several goals in this regard. China promotes the international use of its currency to establish the Renminbi as a global trading currency. This includes initiatives such as creating currency swap agreements with other countries and promoting Yuan-denominated trade agreements. The US has imposed sanctions against China and other countries in recent years that can restrict access to dollar liquidity. Dedollarization is seen as a way to safeguard against such measures. In recent years, China has increasingly sought trade agreements with other nations to encourage trade in national currencies instead of in US dollars. Dedollarization is part of China's strategy to expand its geopolitical power and to develop an alternative financial system that is less dominated by the

US.

The new global alliance would benefit from the creation of new financial instruments or an enhanced role for the euro. It can promote its own reserve currency and safeguard the use of the euro in international trade relations. Creating a robust and stable financial system that is not dependent on the US dollar thus provides a stronger position on the global stage. It will be exciting to see how these geopolitical and economic shifts will affect the global economic order in the coming years.

If the Alliance were to establish its own dedicated funds for infrastructure financing and development initiatives in emerging markets, it could achieve multiple strategic objectives simultaneously. Such funding mechanisms would not only benefit member states by creating new economic opportunities and investment pathways, but also enhance the Alliance's global presence by supporting sustainable development in high-growth regions across Africa, Asia and Latin America.

By investing in projects related to transportation, digital infrastructure, energy access and education, the Alliance could offer a values-based alternative to existing models of development financing, particularly those tied to authoritarian regimes. This would allow partner countries to build their economies without becoming entangled in debt traps or opaque geopolitical dependencies.

Given the rapid expansion of the sustainability sector, the Alliance could further increase its impact by prioritizing green technologies and renewable energy projects. Investments in solar, wind, clean hydrogen, and climate-resilient infrastructure would not only protect the environment, but also reduce long-term energy dependencies, foster technological leadership and promote economic resilience within and beyond the Alliance. In doing so, the Alliance would strengthen both its strategic autonomy and its credibility as a global force for sustainable, inclusive growth, demonstrating that economic progress and environmental responsibility are not mutually exclusive, but deeply intertwined.

If the Alliance were to establish its own dedicated fund for infrastructure financing and development initiatives in emerging markets, it could achieve multiple strategic goals at once. This would not only create new economic opportunities for member states, but also offer partner countries an attractive, transparent alternative to existing initiatives dominated by authoritarian powers.

One of the most prominent examples of such efforts is China's Belt and Road Initiative. a global infrastructure strategy launched in 2013, which has invested in roads, railways, ports, and energy projects across Asia, Africa, and Latin America. While the Belt and Road Initiative has succeeded in building strategic influence for China, it has also drawn criticism for non-transparent lending practices, environmental damage, labor exploitation and creating unsustainable debt burdens in developing nations.

In contrast, an Alliance-led fund could be structured around transparent governance, democratic values, and long-term sustainability. It could invest in clean energy, digital connectivity, public health infrastructure and climate-resilient development, positioning itself as a green and fair pathway to growth for emerging economies. Projects could be carried out in cooperation with local governments and civil society, ensuring ownership and accountability.

Would the Alliance also establish its own financial institutions or banks to pool and manage the financial interests of the member countries, it could also act as a lender in international markets, thereby strengthening its own political and economic position. In the event of geopolitical tensions or economic crises, a strong financial strength also acts as a stabilizing factor for the global economy

18. APPROACHES

A rule-based world order that promotes international cooperation, peacekeeping and the strengthening of political commonalities could create a strong global system. External components such as global trade, finance and peacekeeping provide stability by promoting economic interconnectedness and multilateral cooperation, which in turn reduces global conflict risks. Global trade and finance also act as stabilizers by creating interdependencies between nations. These economic connections can make the cost of conflict too high for any one nation, as disruptions in trade or financial systems can affect all parties involved. Additionally, peacekeeping efforts, when supported by a robust international system, can help resolve conflicts before they escalate into larger-scale violence. A world order grounded in these principles could reduce tensions and foster a more predictable and peaceful global environment.

A new type of alliance between transatlantic, Asian countries and Europe would provide an important platform for multilateral cooperation focusing on technological innovation, economic strength, security cooperation and cultural exchange. By pooling the resources and capabilities of these entities, the alliance could not only promote its members' interests but also exert a positive influence on the global order.

Networks not only strengthen the economic base of the actors involved, but also promote stability and growth. By establishing win-win partnerships, the partners increase their efficiency and reduce potential uncertainties. The future belongs to those who build and use networks effectively, be it through innovation, crisis management or geopolitical stability efforts. Not everyone has really realized this yet. Networks in the form of cultural connections, economic partnerships or digital platforms are the driving force to promote innovation, overcome crises and ensure stability. It is in times of uncertainty and turbulence that the true power of well-established networks becomes apparent. They enable a faster exchange of knowledge, facilitate access to resources and thus act as support systems. Whether in business, culture, or geopolitics, the relationships formed through networks create resilience and flexibility in the face of challenges. In times of uncertainty, networks become even more crucial. They provide channels for rapid communication, help identify solutions faster, and enable organizations or governments to adapt quickly to shifting circumstances.

In order to build effective networks, it is important to act purposefully. They should not be random, but should be geared to specific goals and needs. One should know exactly which resources or information are needed and who is involved in the network. Networks are based not only on pure connection, but on the exchange of added value. Those who help others and provide useful information, resources or support will get more in return in the long run. Networks operate symbiotically, not unilaterally; trust plays a central role in their construction. Relationships need to be nurtured over time and it is important to ask for support not only in emergencies or acute needs, but in continuous competition.

However, not all political actors worldwide are fully aware of the potential of these networks. Some might still operate in silos or resist collaboration due to traditional mindsets, political interests, or concerns about sovereignty. Overcoming these barriers is a key challenge for the future. Creating an inclusive environment where networks are cultivated and expanded across borders, sectors, and cultures will be essential for fostering more resilient and adaptable global systems.

To address these challenges, it is crucial to engage in dialogue and education that highlights the benefits of collaboration and the interconnectedness of global issues. Political actors should be encouraged to participate in cross-sector partnerships that can bridge gaps between various stakeholders, including government, civil society, academia, and the private sector. One effective strategy could be the establishment of platforms or forums that facilitate knowledge sharing and collaboration, allowing diverse actors to come together and explore common goals. These platforms can help break down silos by promoting transparency and trust, which are essential for successful cooperation.

Additionally, fostering a culture of inclusivity and respect for different perspectives can enhance the effectiveness of these networks. This involves recognizing and valuing the contributions of all participants, particularly those from underrepresented communities, and ensuring that their voices are heard in decision-making processes. Investing in capacity-building initiatives can also empower local actors, enabling them to engage more effectively in global networks. By providing resources, training and support, we can equip these actors with the skills and knowledge needed to navigate complex political landscapes and advocate for collaborative approaches. By addressing traditional mindsets and encouraging a shift towards a more collaborative and interconnected way of thinking, we can create a more resilient and adaptable global system that is better equipped to address pressing challenges such as climate change, health crises, and economic inequalities.

It is in times of uncertainty and turbulence that the true power of well-established networks becomes apparent. They enable faster knowledge sharing, access to resources and can act as support systems. These are insights that a president Trump, for example, completely misunderstands. His approach is based on the principle of power-ripping isolation through individual deals, focusing on national advantages and autarky. In his satirical manner, he is generally sceptical about international alliances and multilateral agreements. However, this approach has also highlighted the challenges of an increasingly globalized and interconnected world system. Even if you want to be independent and self-sufficient as a nation, it is difficult to keep up with the global competition; which moves in networks. Whenever the US decouples from global partners, other countries will quickly fill the gap and gain strategic advantages.

Looking at the geopolitical landscape, it quickly becomes clear that stable alliances between countries are crucial to ensure regional as well as global stability. A globally networked and cooperative system counteracts geopolitical tensions, while isolationism potentially leads to more tension and uncertainty. President Trump is ruthlessly trying to whip through the fact that the US only benefits itself through trade agreements and international treaties. It has also lost some of the opportunities to benefit from global cooperation that the US once had and which is so crucial in an increasingly interconnected world.

Donald Trump and networks, that's like oil and water or in other words, like a smartphone without wi-fi, disconnected, glitchy and constantly searching for a signal he's not interested in receiving. Whether it's international alliances, institutional frameworks, or digital ecosystems, networks require trust, cooperation, and long-term thinking, none of which have ever been his strong suit. There is the man who leads the world's largest nation, but at the same time sees the idea of networking with other countries as a weakness. He and his co-ideologists prefer to unite globally with other actors, roaring like the lone wolf in the forest, unfortunately without realizing that the rest of the world has long been working in a much larger, interconnected system, that they simply did not recognize. This attitude to international agreements is trying to empty the vacuum bag by simply pulling the device out of the socket - not a good idea. In the end they turn not only the device, but also the whole room into a mess. Instead of getting their fingers dirty on international relations, they choose to win the diplomatic solo game. The result is a global space in which the US basically shoots itself in the foot, while the rest of the world plans the next step in a marathon of teamwork.

In alliance pacts, the entities jointly represent their interests, which strengthens their negotiating position vis-à-vis third parties. This is particularly important when it comes to significant economic or geopolitical issues. By forming alliances, smaller or less influential states can strengthen their position by joining forces with stronger partners. Larger states also benefit from alliances because they expand their power and influence on the world stage through joint action.

What is needed are strong, large-scale alliances. These are the ones that truly make an impact. Fragmented bilateral agreements, by contrast, tend to weaken and undermine the cohesion of the broader alliance system. Instead of fostering unity and shared strategic direction, they often lead to disjointed efforts, misaligned interests and diluted influence. In today's interconnected world, only comprehensive, multilateral frameworks can provide the stability, coordination, and strategic leverage required to tackle complex global challenges. A patchwork of isolated deals may offer short-term wins, but they erode the long-term effectiveness of any collective effort. Strategic unity must take precedence over piecemeal diplomacy. That is why, when it comes to major initiatives, the guiding principle must be to think big and act boldly, not to make half-hearted efforts. In building systems based on large-scale partnerships, it is essential to invest in economic depth and visionary scope. These strategic alliances must aim not only for short-term gains but for long-term structural impact across broad sectors.

As a basis for stable, long-term cooperation, alliance pacts can prevent conflicts. They provide collective protection, particularly in the field of defence and security. This means that Member States support each other, ensuring the safety of all involved.Bilateral agreements are usually limited to specific issues, while big alliances offer a common foreign policy that helps states to follow a unified line towards other countries.

Alliance pacts reduce the risk of unilateral decisions. They have the potential to maintain long-term stable relationships and reduce conflict. However, their effectiveness depends heavily on the concrete design and continuous commitment of the partners involved.

Creating a shared interest, especially in a hesitant initial phase, requires sensitivity, clear communication and convincing added value for all involved. From a tentative approach, an intense and productive relationship develops when some crucial conditions are met. In the initial phase, it is important to communicate transparently about the goals and possible benefits of cooperation. Open communication, in which the needs and expectations of all sides are heard and respected, lays the foundation for a strong relationship. Trust is the glue that forms a strong, productive network from an initial skepticism.

The aim is to identify areas where there are overlaps in the partners' goals and interests. When all sides recognize their individual strengths and weaknesses and clearly identify the synergies between their skills and resources, a sense of common direction arises. Instead of falling into a competitive mindset, the focus should be on the advantages of competitive cooperation that promise individual benefits without overvaluing others. To turn a timid approach into something productive, it is advisable to start with small but successful initiatives. These strengthen confidence and increase the willingness to take on more responsibility. First, straightforward cooperation from which all parties benefit equally creates win-win situations and is the basis for long-term and deeper partnerships. One of the strongest levers for more intensive cooperation is knowledge exchange. By providing access to new perspectives as a partner, you naturally deepen trust and cooperation. As all participants learn from the collaboration, a long-term interest in building this relationship arises.

The responsibility for the success and failure of a

partnership is ideally shared. It is not just about acting as a partner, but as equal co-creators of a larger vision. After all, one wants to keep the future-oriented advantages in mind. Trust in a partnership grows when everyone sees that they can not only benefit from it in the short term, but also emerge stronger and more stable from cooperation in the future.

A shared vision for the future that leaves room for growth and further development, motivates to work intensively on the relationship. Often, decision-makers are afraid to go new ways or allow changes because they feel there are obstacles or too much unknown. Why not new partnerships? Sticking to old ways of thinking and hesitant approaches means that you miss opportunities. The subjects request offers and ask if they really have the courage to commit themselves together. Then it's time to make nails with heads. The willingness to take responsibility, try new things and be ready to roll up your sleeves is crucial in such moments. Determination is not only a prerequisite for success, but also for overcoming resistance and dealing with uncertainties. What is the value of creative thinking or a bold vision? Even if it does not lead to the desired result, the process of dealing with the idea and trying out the opportunities was still enriching. And if not realized, it was a nice creative dream that was worth to be lived once. It's like an adventure where you discover, learn and grow. And who knows, maybe the creative dream will become the seed for something else that later blossoms unexpectedly. In the end it was at least a journey that you started with courage and openness and that is already a success.

Who now claims the factual? It is simply necessary, otherwise one could not travel to new horizons. In order to achieve it, it is essential that we do not let ourselves be guided by illusions or mere assumptions, but recognize the facts and act on them. Without the perception of actual conditions, any change, any progression into the unknown is fraught with a high risk because one does not build on a solid foundation. Those who make use of the facts accept reality and are able not only to recognize the difficulties, but also to identify the best possibilities.

Without a solid foundation of facts and a clear perception of reality, it would be difficult to set the course or make informed decisions. But the facts alone are not enough to enable innovation and progress. It is the combination of facts and the willingness to deal with them creatively. By taking facts as a starting point, you move safely on solid ground and still have to be brave enough to break new ground. The balance between acknowledging reality and seeing the future is what makes the difference.

Who will take responsibility? Who has the courage to put the factual in the foreground without being held back by fear of the unknown? It takes a mixture of pragmatism and vision to realize that facts are not the end of thinking, but the basis for what can come. The journey to new horizons begins when you take the facts seriously and then courageously go on to expand the limits of what is known.

Major changes or innovations require a leap into the unknown where you cannot know at any moment what the outcome will be. But it is precisely this courage, the confidence in one's vision and the willingness to take risks that is the spark that ignites the adventure. Timidity not only slows one's own development, but also prevents the world from benefiting from new ideas and perspectives. Remarkable discoveries and progress have never been made by hesitating or waiting for the perfect moment, but by action that has set the course in spite of all uncertainties and doubts.

Surely, the realization of a breathtaking new alliance would not be a charlatan epic. The efforts to explore would be great, if not gigantic. Anyone who dares to go that far must bring a certain measure of resilience, determination and above all a deep conviction into their own vision. It requires visionaries who are willing not to give up even in the face of adversity, but to draw a lesson from every stumbling block. These state leaders are not only innovators, but also risk-takers who enter unknown lands, even if the path to them is anything but easy. So there are always those who dare, who have the urge to go beyond the ordinary. And often it is precisely these actors who end up paving the way for others and setting new standards. Even if the road is rocky and difficult, they will be the ones who will eventually reap the fruits of their efforts and the world will change thanks to their courage and perseverance.

The "kibitze", that is, those who stand on the edge and watch, wonder at every little detail. They will indeed not come out of amazement. Those who are not actually in the game and just observe things develop a mixture of astonishment, criticism and of course curiosity. But they are not the makers. While the brave players take the cards in hand, venture into unknown terrain, the observers stand there and analyze every risk and every decision. They have their own comforts and safer places from which to comment on events. Could political players also be among them? In their eyes, everything is a spectacular adventure, a grandiose showdown that also gives them a thrill.

It takes visionaries, but also network engineers, strategy jugglers, and utility analysts to complete the mosaic. Perhaps great secrets are still being dug out from the depths of political star managers. These diverse roles, from strategic planning to precise risk-benefit analysis, are the quiet but crucial forces that everything works. They bring the vision down to earth, transform ambitions into actionable strategies, and always maintain a clear overview. Sometimes the truly important insights or hidden treasures of political power only come to light when courageous actors pool their expertise.

Emotional cultural inclusion requires the ability to understand the needs and concerns of cultures and to consider their individual values. This creates a sense of participation and responsibility. The cultural differences in the patterns of alliance pacts are therefore deeply rooted in the respective social norms and values. A successful alliance must therefore not only be based on the hard facts and economic aspects, but also develop a fine sense of cultural differences and how partners interact with each other. Understanding these cultural nuances is crucial to creating long-term, stable and effective alliances.

Trust is the foundation of any political partnership and when time is often a critical factor, this trust must be built quickly. Psychological connections arise not only through words, but also through authenticity and a genuine interest in the partner. In many successful alliances, it is not necessarily the long period of cooperation that makes the difference, but the ability to build an emotional bridge within a very short time.

Thus, the first encounter in an alliance, the first impression, the ability to listen to each other and the willingness to engage with one another are already the foundation for everything that follows. In a world that is increasingly shaped by technology and distance, this psychic connection can be nurtured even more strongly through authentic communication and the exchange of visionary ideas and common goals.

The desired safety ensures that all participants act more openly and cooperatively. Trust is then quickly established not only through positive expectations, but also through the fact that all participants operate in a protected space where their concerns are heard and respected. The true connection goes beyond mere contracts and agreements. It is about creating emotional resonance that ensures that the partners not only communicate rationally with each other, but are also in harmony on the communicative level. Shared values, a shared vision and the desire to shape the same future create this strong emotional bond that drives an alliance.

Another prerequisite for building a fast psychological connection is to try out common challenges and share successes with each other. This strengthens the sense of belonging and gives all participants the confidence that they can achieve more together. Once this connection is established, even difficult decisions and complex situations can be mastered with more ease, as all partners feel that they are there for each other. The link for strategic alliances in international politics is first and foremost the common interest and mutual goals that the partners connect to each other. This requires constant communication, trust, flexibility and adherence to shared values. When these elements are taken into account, alliances can not only exist but also remain successful in changing geopolitical landscapes and achieve common goals in the long term.

The success rate in questioning thoughts and needs depends not only on rationality and clear communication, but also on the cultural intelligence of the participants as well as the ability to create a relationship of trust. In an ideal scenario where all these factors work well together, the hit rate can be set high. However, when obstacles such as misunderstandings, lack of empathy or cultural differences come into play, it will be significantly lower.

Thought transfer in international partnerships could be understood as a metaphor for an ideal, almost magical communication between countries or political actors. Instead of communicating only through words or formal channels, countries could understand each other directly and without misunderstandings, intuitively and in a deep, empathetic exchange. This idea evokes a longing for a kind of diplomacy that goes beyond the traditional means and is based on better understanding and a stronger common feeling.

Intuition and the understanding of togetherness are becoming increasingly important. Countries that are able to develop the magical ability to recognize the ideas of others without long words could indeed gain the decisive advantage in international relations. It is not only what is said, but also how it is said and how deep the mutual understanding reaches. It may be that you will remember the times when you did not know what to do with the first ideas of the alliance and then the doors were opened to an epochal communication. The arsenal of feedback will appear to be enormous. It would be exciting to learn more about the specific aspects of this alliance that has emerged. What were the main issues or goals? Which challenges had to be overcome? And how have the feedback processes developed over time?

A crucial element in this continuous dialogue is the ability to use "socio-political mirror neurons". The conversation partners also reflect each other's thoughts and the intentional meaning. This creates a space for deeper cognitive connections that go beyond mere exchange of facts. If this process takes place in a global alliance or transnational collaboration, it could lead to a collective intuition and a global consciousness that becomes more sophisticated over time.

All the participants in an alliance must constantly keep in mind what the great lines of the alliance look like. It must be clear how decisions are made and what roles each partner has, is there a common body? What are the partners' decision-making powers? A clear value system, transparent structures and binding targets help to steer partnerships in the right direction.

Each of the world's regions is conditioned to a multitude of stimuli, which must be addressed and brought to a common denominator. An alliance is only viable if it is based on a clearly defined governance structure that regulates the powers of the partners transparently. Binding targets, a shared value system and transparent structures are crucial. The challenge is to define the roles of each partner so that the alliance as a whole remains strong, while also preserving individual interests and powers. This makes the cooperation not only stable, but also efficient and trusting in the long term.

In many regions, economic advantages are a decisive

factor. These include trade agreements, access to markets, infrastructure projects and the possibility of sharing resources. Regions like Asia or Europe often pursue geopolitical interests such as access to strategic resources or protection from external threats. These interests are found in the military alliances for supra-regional security. In Africa or South America, for example, the focus could be on cultural cooperation and promoting social cohesion. In certain regions, the Pacific island states or North and Central Africa, climate protection and environmental policy would be a primary incentive.

The alliance policy on a global scale therefore requires the skillful addressing of specific regional stimuli. This means that the alliance integrates the economic, geopolitical, cultural and ecological needs of each region and tends towards an extension of the common vision. A flexible framework and constant dialogue are needed to bring the different needs together in order to make the alliance successful in the long term.

And then you should consider what contributes to the mutual trust building. The sum of political experiences needs to be thoroughly examined, but then you know where you stand. Building trust is the foundation of any successful alliance. Trust is the glue that holds the different partners together, especially in such a complex and diverse international partnership. It is about understanding the political experiences of the different actors, making use of historical lessons and knowing how to position oneself in the geopolitical reality. Rational evaluations evaluate and determine the professional interaction.

By thoroughly analyzing each partner's historical background, political goals and behavior patterns, you get a clearer picture of where you really are. When open and transparent communication is established and trust is gradually gained through constructive cooperation, a stable foundation is created on which the alliance can thrive in the long term. If everyone understands what you are, it is the best conditions for successful cooperation.

When all parties have a clear understanding of each other's identities, values, and goals, it creates the optimal environment for collaboration. This understanding minimizes misunderstandings and enhances coordination, enabling partners to work together more effectively toward shared objectives. Ultimately, a well-established alliance, grounded in trust and mutual understanding, is more likely to achieve long-term success. Long-term success in any partnership hinges on this trust and mutual understanding, as it encourages open communication and adaptability in the face of challenges. In essence, investing time in building these relationships pays off by creating a resilient and dynamic alliance that can navigate complexities together.

19. NEW TONES OF A FUTURE MUSIC

If we imagine a scenario in which some of the current heads of state and government might no longer be in power in five years, we are faced with a picture of interesting and potentially chaotic phenomena.Will the Kremlin suddenly be a free field of speculation and intrigue? It's like a poker game where everyone puts their chips on the table, but no one can be sure whether the next bet will actually be revealed or end in a gigantic coup d'état.

Perhaps the Kremlin will become an arena of battle royale, with oligarchs, secret service chiefs and military leaders fighting for power, while at the same time the country turns into a political hullabaloo that ends in a race to see who will continue to lead the next, legitimized dictatorship. In the end, we may get another Putin back, using the system to his advantage under the guise of a new era, but with any doubters silenced.

The rise of a new Chinese dragon could also mark a historic moment in which the Communist Party seeks either an authoritarian successor or an uncharted transition to a slightly more open society. Since Xi Jinping was considered infallible, it could well be that the party is suddenly confronted with pressure from outside and inside to reorient itself. This could possibly be through more freedom for the regions, economic reforms or even an opening up of society. On the other hand, the tendency to control could also improve. In the midst of this unrest, the new dragon would suddenly take control again with an iron fist, only without the same charm of a treacherously smiling Xi.

Donald Trump could even continue to divide public opinion as a kind of showman of the political circus and stir up American politics with his announcements. Perhaps he would be omnipresent in the media landscape as the "Voice of America", even if he is officially no longer in power. New scandals, questionable statements and alternative facts would continue to be his trademark. The shifts in power could lead to a world in which chaos reigns or space is found for new ideas, movements or political systems. Is there more than just the old battle between democracy and authoritarianism? It could also be that more women take the lead. Or there could even be non-traditional, participatory forms of government.

In any case, speculating about who might succeed whom and where would be rmere guesswork. There are simply too many imponderables and constantly changing factors. It is difficult to predict who exactly will take over, be it through internal power struggles, elections or political upheaval. Especially in authoritarian systems, where succession arrangements are often obscured or do not exist at all, it remains a hot topic full of uncertainty.

Nevertheless, it is clear that, given all the constellations, it makes sense to at least consider the prospects of a new type of alliance organization. Thinking about the formation of new alliances and strategic partnerships would not be a bad idea. A perspective could emerge that will require even more strength in the future, especially if the existing political leadership constellations change. A business-as-usual approach is hardly sustainable in today's, let alone tomorrow's, geopolitical landscape. Global challenges, from economic shifts to security threats and ecological crises, will require a realignment of international relations and alliances. In interdependent systems, clinging to outdated power structures would not only be ineffective, but also destabilizing.

Traditional alliances, often rooted in historical contexts and rigid power dynamics, may struggle to address the multifaceted challenges we face today. As global interdependencies deepen, a more flexible and adaptive approach to collaboration is essential. The emergence of new geopolitical players and the shifting priorities of existing ones call for a reevaluation of how nations interact. Economic instability, security threats, and environmental crises are not isolated issues; they are interconnected challenges that transcend borders. In this context, a business-as-usual mindset is inadequate. Nations must be willing to forge innovative partnerships that prioritize collective problem-solving over rigid loyalty to outdated alliances.

This perspective encourages a more dynamic approach to international relations, one that embraces diversity in partnerships and encourages collaboration across sectors, government, private industry, and civil society. By harnessing the strengths and capabilities of different stakeholders, we can create more resilient alliances that are better equipped to respond to the complexities of our time.

The global economic landscape is already fundamentally unsettled. The aspirations of Western nations for free trade and global integration are being put to the test by populist movements, protectionist tendencies and trade wars. For many countries, it might make more sense to rely less on traditional Western markets and more on regional partnerships or alternative trade routes.

If China intervenes even more in the global security architecture and Russia increasingly asserts itself as a geopolitical player, this could put global security alliances to the test. In any case, the free West would have to unite more closely. Governments everywhere could orient themselves according to their similar world views, which would challenge them to reshape their alliances. Democracies could focus on shared values, ranging from the rule of law and human rights to economic justice, and unite in a new bloc. At the same time, autocratic states could solidarize into even more violence.

Moreover, as political leadership evolves, new opportunities for collaboration may arise. Emerging leaders may bring fresh perspectives and priorities that can reshape existing alliances or inspire the formation of entirely new ones. It is crucial for nations to remain open to these possibilities, recognizing that adaptability will be key in maintaining stability and fostering cooperation in an unpredictable world.

In the 21st century, alliances are managed in different ways, with the dynamics changing dramatically due to technological and economic changes. Thanks to modern communication technologies, alliances can be effectively coordinated worldwide without geographical barriers. Social media platforms, video calls, instant messaging and cloud tools enable fast and efficient communication between partners. Data will be analyzed as quickly as possible to feed into strategic decisions that strengthen alliances. Artificial intelligence will help to identify risks and predict future trends, enabling optimal proactive collaboration.

The alliances have become so flexible that they even form temporary unifications as required in order to respond to current challenges. On the one hand, increasing flexibility can bring advantages through rapid reactions, but on the other hand it can also create uncertainty and instability. This poses a major threat to the stability of the structures that are needed as a backbone. Nevertheless, the impression remains that strong alliances are asserting themselves as an option without alternative in the competition between the major global powers such as the USA, China and Russia. This is particularly the case when tensions over strategic adjustments urgently demand it.

If alliances do not remain anchored in the long term, it will probably be due to a lack of mutual trust. As a result, countries will distance themselves from one another. Such insecure partnerships cause positions to constantly fluctuate, which leads to uncertainty and instability in the long term. If alliances are formed mainly out of the need to respond to current threats in the short term, their objectives have not been clearly defined from the outset. They are therefore not very sustainable in the long term.

The cement is not only joint military strength, but also

soft power, such as culture and diplomacy. The concept of soft power was developed by the neoliberal political scientist Joseph Samuel Nye as a way of maturing people and nations through cultural and political activity. He argued for more multilateralism on the international stage. In his opinion, it is the system of "soft power" that prevents terrorism from gaining followers again and again and that should also be able to balance out the global differences between nations. If alliances are to be kept attractive, these aspects should not be ignored.

One aspect that perhaps still receives too little attention in the current debate is the area of climate change and ecological responsibility. States are increasingly beginning to forge alliances on this basis. This involves linking economic and security policy interests. Such alliances could form a new global bloc centered around the creation of a sustainable global economy. The question of access to resource-rich areas and the fight for water rights are also a starting point for international coalitions. Countries that are particularly affected by climate change must join forces to find global solutions to these existential threats.

The changes we are experiencing today require a rethink of political, economic and social structures. In the modern world, it is not enough to simply react casually to possible scenarios. Pro-active, concrete solutions are required to meet the new global challenges. It is not just about acting in the short term, but also about developing visions for the future. They must be able to keep pace with the changes on the world stage. Global politics, economics and security are moving in a new direction, and those who are not prepared in good time run the risk of being left behind.

The form of such a completely new multilateral alliance would have the added benefit of strengthening European cohesion. Just imagine what could emerge from this unity. How Europe positions itself under these conditions depends on the scenario of new partnerships. In any case, targeted measures are needed immediately so that it is not too late for visions.

May European societies be spared the fearfulness of political leaders. Fearfulness is the worst of the negative influences on political management. When political leaders are guided by fear, their decisions will be hesitant, incoherent and uninspiring. This in turn has an impact on the stability and ability to act of a country or region.

Leaders who are beset by fear find it difficult to develop and communicate a clear and convincing vision. A leadership that is characterized by uncertainty and doubt finds it difficult to inspire society and gain its trust. In times of major upheaval, it is particularly important for leadership to set a clear direction. Good leadership in a dynamically globalized world requires decisions to be made that are associated with risks. A leader who is characterized by fear may not be willing to take risks that may be necessary to achieve long-term benefits. Without a willingness to take risks, the potential for innovation and progress remains untapped.

Courageous leadership does not mean taking risks blindly, but rather acting with foresight and a clear plan, even if the future is uncertain, unless you simply want to walk into the storm with a casual shrug of the shoulders while ignoring the weather forecast. In uncertain times, it is decisive and forward-looking decisions that lead to long-term stability and success. Political leaders must therefore also have a certain psychological resilience in order to withstand the pressure and uncertainty of responsibility. An anxiety-free, self-assured leadership contributes to a more stable environment and promotes shared commitments. Don't let up, don't stagger around in uncertainty, but keep at it, analyze and act together.

A new Atlantic-Pacific Alliance including Europe would need to closely coordinate its military, economic and diplomatic efforts. By pooling the resources and strategic advantages of its members, the alliance could effectively counter the growing influence of Russia,

China, Iran, and North Korea. Ultimately, it would involve creating a coherent response to the geopolitical challenges posed by these countries while fostering alternative models of international order that promote stability, freedom, and cooperation.

One of the most critical pillars of such an alliance would be integrated military planning and joint military exercises. These are not optional additions, but an essential prerequisite for preparing member states for hybrid and conventional threats, including cyber warfare, disinformation campaigns, and conventional military aggression. They improve interoperability between the armed forces of different continents, enable rapid deployment and coordinated responses in times of crisis, strengthen deterrence by demonstrating unity and readiness, and thus raise the cost to any potential aggressor.

Beyond defense, the alliance should have the potential to generate significant economic benefits. Robust and diversified trade networks should reduce strategic dependence on China and other authoritarian economies. it offers the view to joint innovations in critical sectors, such as artificial intelligence, clean energy, biotechnology, semiconductor manufacturing including space exploration to secure technological leadership.

The concept of the trans-oceanic alliance as outlined here goes far beyond a mere informal forum. It deliberately distances itself from the idea of an exclusive club and instead positions itself as a joint endeavor grounded in shared legitimacy. This framing suggests a commitment to inclusivity, transparency and collective responsibility on the global stage. The focus is on operationalizing norms, not as abstract values, but as tools for situational problem-solving in key policy areas such as climate change, global poverty, food security, and education. In this sense, the alliance appears to be envisioned as a pragmatic actor, capable of translating shared principles into actionable strategies. At its core is a security platform that combines crisis response and crisis prevention. This approach reflects a profound understanding of global interdependence and the need for reactive and proactive governance capacities.

Perhaps most notable is the characterization of the Alliance as a pact, a framework not only for the preparation but also for the active implementation of a planned yet adaptable political management strategy. This suggests a model that combines strategic foresight with tactical flexibility, a rare but increasingly necessary quality given today's complex global challenges.

What to do if such a concept doesn't work consensually? It's a critical question, especially if the ambition behind such a concept is to be taken seriously. If the trans-oceanic alliance fails to function on the basis of consensus, there isn't sufficient political will or shared normative ground. There are still several strategic paths forward, depending on which core goals are to be preserved. Instead of relying on full consensus, a core group of committed states could move ahead with concrete initiatives. These pilot projects could serve as models and eventually create momentum to attract others.

Or the concept could be designed in a modular way, breaking it down into specific policy areas for example climate, food security, education, allowing different configurations of actors to cooperate based on interest and capacity. This keeps the overall framework flexible and functional. Perhaps the failure of consensus stems from legitimacy deficits or poor communication. In this case, the question must be asked why consensus is lacking. Is there distrust, conflicting interests, or unclear benefit-sharing? The answer might lie in bridge-building diplomacy, paired with transparent communication and inclusive design processes. A lack of consensus doesn't necessarily mean the project fails. Instead, it could mark the beginning of a more flexible, adaptive strategy. Global governance in the 21st century is rarely consensual in the traditional sens, but it can still be effective if it's dynamic, learning-oriented and inclusive.

As the number of global actors and policy areas grows, the need for streamlined and strategic international policy management becomes ever more urgent. Complexity demands clarity.With more stakeholders and topics on the table, only well-structured international policy coordination can ensure effective outcomes. Multilateralism without focus risks paralysis. A concise political management framework is essential when many players and diverse issues are in play.

This expansion in stakeholders and policy domains makes one thing clear: effective international cooperation cannot rely on improvisation. It needs structure, strategy, and clarity.Without a streamlined framework, multilateralism can quickly become gridlocked. The more voices at the table, the greater the risk of fragmentation, duplication, or even paralysis. Consensus becomes harder to achieve, and implementation more difficult to coordinate.

Complexity, if unmanaged, undermines impact.

It's not about oversimplification, but about intelligent orchestration, setting priorities, clarifying roles, aligning timelines and ensuring accountability. In such a framework, flexibility and planning are not contradictions, but complementary. Adaptive mechanisms must operate within strategic parameters.The future of multilateralism depends not just on goodwill, but on governance design. Effective outcomes require intentional coordination, based on shared principles, pragmatic tools, and the readiness to act together.

Comparative platforms play a crucial role in monitoring and analyzing power dynamics across the spheres of economics, research, and military affairs.Their function is not merely observational, they provide the strategic intelligence needed to understand shifting balances of influence and to anticipate structural transformations at the global level. Whether in the form of think tanks, intergovernmental observatories, or transnational research consortia, these platforms act as early warning systems, knowledge hubs and policy advisors all at once. In an era marked by multipolar competition, technological disruption, and hybrid threats, such platforms are indispensable. They help policymakers of alliances to distinguish between noise and signal, identifying which developments are tactical fluctuations, and which represent systemic shifts in global power structures.

Interest monitoring is most effective when grounded in evidence-based evaluation. In an international environment shaped by complex interdependencies and competing agendas, strategic observation must go beyond intuition or political assumption. It requires data, methodology and critical reflection. Whether in tracking alliances, investment flows, research priorities or military deployments, only evidence-based analysis can reveal patterns that matter and distinguish between superficial trends and fundamental shifts. This triad -

what, how and when - forms the backbone of any effective evaluation framework. Without it, policies in an alliance remain speculative. This makes governance both accountable and adaptable.

A democratic alliance must demonstrate that it can offer efficiency without authoritarian shortcuts, solidarity without ideological rigidity, and resilience without centralization of power. The contrast with autocratic blocs, often faster in decision-making but weaker in accountability, underscores the importance of building systems that combine legitimacy with capability. In this context, clarity in interests, structured evaluation, and responsive governance are not technicalities, they are strategic necessities.

An "APTO"- alliance, as described here as a model, aims to provide its members with long-term stability in the global order, economic systems, financial markets, and scientific progress. At its core, the alliance is based on values such as democracy, transparency, participation, accountability and the rule of law, principles that are not merely political in nature but also essential for resilient and sustainable international cooperation. The initiative brings together key players from politics, business, the military, science and civil society to promote dialogue, develop educational initiatives and create frameworks that optimize decision-making processes at all levels of international politics. A common security policy would be the foundation and necessary prerequisite for an effective counterweight to antagonistic blocs of autocratic major powers. An APTO Alliance strives for more stable, inclusive and future-oriented cooperation and would well fill the above mentioned geographical „horseshoe" stretching from the Atlantic to the Pacific with Europe as its anchor point.

ABOUT THE AUTHOR

J-G Matuszek

Educated at the universities of Innsbruck, Perugia, and Salzburg, J-G. Matuszek holds advanced degrees in Language Sciences, Political Science, Empirical System Sciences, International Relations, Communication Sciences, and Philosophy. His postgraduate studies include qualifications in marketing, corporate communications, management, innovation, and development strategies. He is also a certified business consultant.

His multifaceted career spans roles as a translator, interpreter, high school teacher, and journalist. He has held senior management positions in multinational corporations and worked as a consultant and coach for mid-sized enterprises, focusing on international management, marketing, and human resources. He has served on the boards of various companies in Germany and Switzerland and held leadership roles in corporate certification companies.

Matuszek is a board member of the Swiss foundation "Globility-Circle" and a guest lecturer at several universities and business schools. In addition to his academic and corporate achievements, he pursued a parallel career in athletics, serving as President of the Austrian Taekwondo Federation. He has also led innovative collaborations at the intersection of high-performance diagnostics, business, and sport.

BOOKS OF THE AUTHOR

NEW VALUE ECONOMY - Manager quo vadis?   ISBN 9783981263206

MANAGEMENT DER NACHHALTIGKEIT   ISBN 9783658022891

SPORT FÜR MANAGER   ISBN 9783658036379

MANAGEMENT DER POLITIK - EUROPA   ISBN 9783990108529

EUROPÄISCH DENKEN   ISBN 9783738625592

EUROPÄISCH HANDELN   ISBN 9783750414501

MANAGEMENT VERSUS SPIRITUALITÄT?   ISBN 9783854314501

RUF NACH DEM SINN   ISBN 9783748144199

MUT ZUM SINN   ISBN 9783750418943

KICKOFF ZUM SINN   ISBN 9783752690200

MANAGEMENT SET-UP   ISBN 9783751941884

DER MANAGER *Roman*   ISBN 9783752648911

REFLEXIONEN Lyrik   ISBN 9783752603866

DIE TAEKWONDO MATRIX   ISBN 9783754352571

THE TAEKWONDO MATRIX   ISBN 9783754395394

TAEKWONDO MATRIX - SPORT EFFIZIENZ   ISBN 9783758307423

EVALUIEREN   ISBN 9783756228805

PSYCHE DER WELTGESCHICHTE   ISBN 9783757810108

POLITIK @ GLOBALE WELT . INTL   ISBN 9783758307942

POLITICS @ GLOBAL – WORLD . INTL   ISBN 9783759706041

THE EUROPE CODE   ISBN 9783759787170

 DER EUROPA CODE   ISBN 9783759708182

PARTEIEN - QUELLEN DES UNSINNS   ISBN 9783769355505

EUROPAS HOFFNUNG ALLIANZEN   ISBN 9783769355505

INTERKONNEKTIVITÄT   ISBN 9783759779687

INTERCONNECTIVITY   ISBN 9783759793485

INTERCONNECTIVITÉ   ISBN 9783769321777

© 2025 J-G Matuszek
Verlag: BoD · Books on Demand GmbH,
Überseering 33, 22297 Hamburg, bod@bod.de
Druck: Libri Plureos GmbH, Friedensallee 273,
22763 Hamburg
ISBN: 978-3-8192-9600-0